RESTORE YOUR FUTURE
A Profit Guide To Renovation

Markley Lee Jones
Jack B. Curry, Jr.
Shirley F. Curry

Curry-Jones Publishers
2717 Devine Street
Columbia, South Carolina
29205

Editor, Kathleen Lewis Sloan
Foreword, Diane Mason
Design, James Flournoy Holmes
Photographer, Mike Hawkins
Illustrations, Janet S. Holmes

Library of Congress Cataloging in Publication Data

Jones, Markley Lee, 1938-
Restore Your Future

Includes index.
1. Buildings--Repair and reconstruction.
2. Dwellings--Remodeling. I. Curry, Jack B., Jr.,1942-
joint author. II. Curry, Shirley F., 1942- joint
author. III. Title.
TH3401.J66   690'.83'0286   80-27820
ISBN 0-9604296-0-3

Acknowledgments—Special writers: Mrs. Diane Mason, Mr. Bob Rowland; Manuscript readers: Mrs. Elizabeth Jones, Mrs. Dorothy Curry, Dr. Rhea T. Workman, Dr. David Bowden, Mrs. Diann Brooks, Mrs. Susan E. Bridwell, Dr. Robert E. Alexander, Ms. Nadia Rasheed, Mr. Jim Pittman, Mr. Dan Dinwiddie, and Mrs. Diane Mason, who also assisted the authors in a thousand other ways; Transcribers: Mrs. Diann Brooks and Mrs. Mary Steffens, who provided valued typing and seemingly endless reviews.

A special every day dedication
to our families

Foreword

What do you see when you look at an aging, rundown house? Do you look beyond the flaking paint and the rusted gutters and see a Pygmalion? Do you see a spacious classic residence awaiting your creative touch? Are you sparked by a sense of history, and wish you could save this old house? Do you see the lath and quality master craftsmanship hiding behind the faded, peeling wallpaper and the delicately carved mouldings underneath the multi-coats of cracked paint?

Do you see dollar signs?

If any of these reactions figure predominately in your thinking, you are a good candidate for home renovation/restoration.

You may be attracted to an older home for your family to restore and live in forever. You may want to see how renovation suits you, and to discover if you can turn this into a profitable vocation. You may be looking for a rewarding side investment. You may see yourself heading toward a permanent career as a home or structural renovator. In any case, you are probably looking for intrinsic rewards as well as monetary ones, and a healthy portion of both. Where do you begin?

You can start by following in the footsteps of Lee Jones and Shirley and Jack Curry, who turned the renovation of one old house into a thriving,well-known business. Their experiences can both inspire and guide you through the ins and outs of home restoration toward the creation of a marvelous residence and the opportunity to earn money in an individual or commercial enterprise.

Since its formation in 1976, the partnership of Curry-Jones has renovated and resold at substantial profit over twenty houses. Most of these renovations were accomplished in very short periods of time.

The first house that Lee, Shirley and Jack acquired was a small and modest structure of about 950-square-feet. It was purchased for $16,500 and after a three-month renovation project, sold for nearly twice that amount. Two years later, in March of 1978, another Curry-Jones home was pictured on the cover of the *Sandlapper Magazine*, with a feature article inside entitled "Miracle at Laurel and Marion."

The authors' former professional backgrounds and their college degrees in business provided little of the "education" they needed for the challenges that awaited them when they first visited the Laurel and Marion address. There were no "how to" books to tell them how to evict the cloister of derelicts who had been camping in the abandoned house for several years, and who were not anxious to surrender their haven. There were two huge holes in the roof, and water damage from rain had completely destroyed the plaster walls and the entire plumbing system. The electrical wiring was shot. The stench was oppressive. And there was enough trash and broken bottles to fill a caravan of garbage trucks.

It took three weeks of daily police visits to clear the home of its former denizens. Sub-contractors were called, but when they arrived they stuck their heads in the door, took one look and a quick sniff and said: "Clean it up and **then** call me—but no promises." Shirley, Jack and Lee plunged into the clean-up operation.

And so it began. As the three novice renovators worked, they learned. They learned how to be handymen. They learned when not to be handymen — when to call in professionals. They learned when to repair, when to tear out and replace. They learned how to supervise work crews. They learned the names of dependable contractors, and the names of ones to avoid. They learned each other's strengths. Jack and Lee were better with financial matters and tools; Shirley had a flair for decorating, accounting, and keeping track of details. Each respected and acquiesced to the others' fortes. All agreed that professional standards of excellence were to be the ultimate goals.

Eventually they learned enough to write a book. This one.

In **Restore Your Future**, Lee, Shirley and Jack share their methods and expertise, creating a model and a guide for you, the profit-minded renovator.

What is true in Columbia, South Carolina, is no doubt true in any town or city in the country. That is, despite much callous destruction, there are still many old homes and buildings left to be renovated. And, as was quoted in the *Sandlapper Magazine*: "Maybe the best thing Columbia [or your town] has is what it's already got." The task now is to find a way to merge the past with the future.

Is there a Laurel and Marion in your town? If so, there may be a "miracle" in your future.

Diane Mason

v

RESTORE YOUR FUTURE
A Profit Guide To Renovation

Preface

During the past two decades and, most especially, since inflation has soared, there has been an increasing interest in older homes and in preserving them. This "craze for nostalgia" has not been confined solely to houses; it has included other structures that might be turned into dwelling places or made useful for those in the professions or various other kinds of businesses (even a chapel into a restaurant and a warehouse into a grocery store).

That is not all: people have simply grown tired of the modern, box-like domiciles with not enough room, too few graceful appointments, and little character. Today's market in older houses is an expression for space, love of the unusual design, and solid construction. Price is not always the criterion; practical and aesthetic reasons coincide. Also, many people deplore the architectural rape of the cities "for progress," the litter-strewn rural landscape, the loss of century-old trees, and mass-produced dwellings. They are anxious for a revival of good taste in architecture, a renewal of the decorative arts, and comfortable, spacious living.

Through renovation, adaptation or restoration, generally the ultimate can be a nice home, in a good location, at a lower cost. You can do-it-yourself or take advantage of a business firm that will do or has already done it for you.

The time for house renovation/restoration was never quite so propitious. Even lending institutions have become aware of the fact that restoration makes good "business sense," and in the near future you will likely see more loans made to individuals and/or business-renovation firms than will go into, for instance, sprawling shopping centers.

Contrast the current photographs, the stunning vitality and beauty of the renovated house, with those of yesterday that reflect the rubble, overgrown yards, broken windows, sagging porches and the overall sad appearance.

The fifteen chapters outline in precise detail practically everything to learn about building-renovation/restoration through a step-by-step process from how best to select a structure, how much you should pay for it, and what expenses and experiences you will avoid.

The advice is applicable to anyone who wishes to renovate a house to occupy as his own residence, or to that individual/investor or business firm which might wish to establish a commercial enterprise. The text is filled with instructive, profitable guidelines.

Every locality contains structures that need renovation—those that would help restore a neighborhood, or would add "flavor" to a community.

K.L.S.

Contents

Ready To Renovate

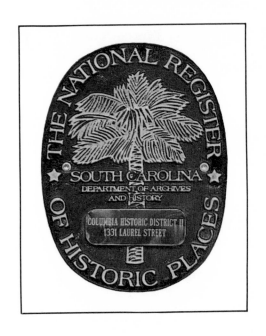

RESTORE YOUR FUTURE
A Profit Guide To Renovation

Selecting The Property

1 Are You A Renovator?

Renovators are similar to people who like antiques. They may refinish furniture or strip old brass objects in their spare time. They admire intricate mouldings on walls and doors even if these do gather dust and take longer to paint. They prefer plastered walls and solid doors, are comfortable in old cellars, and intrigued by stone foundations. They like space-high ceilings and wide hallways, and can recognize beauty and charm long before they notice the musty smell. They imagine how life was in past eras and are committed to providing visual memories of those eras for all to see and enjoy.

Give yourself this sample test. The next time you pass an aging, dilapidated building, house, school or storefront, pause for a moment; reflect upon your reaction. Do you contemplate a modern, efficient structure that could be built on the space occupied by the ruin? Or, does the horror of demolition creep into your mind? Do you visualize the masterpiece that once stood proudly, one whose classic features and stately design reflect a great heritage? Are you inspired to preserve and protect this memento of the architectural past?

If you answered "yes" to the last two questions, you have the prime requisites for becoming a renovator. You are idealistic, sentimental, and a historic "patriot." In your hands, and others like you, rest the horizon of the future and the glory of the past.

How is your business acumen? Do you operate your daily affairs in a business-like way?

To be a successful renovator requires a combination of sensitivity to antiquity and a twentieth-century profit motivation. It could be that you are a philanthropist who only collects and restores antique houses for the benefit of the community. On the other hand, most people who consider renovation do so with the idea of personal gratification and personal profit. Some are individuals who are already investing or would like to invest in real estate and wish to do something creative with their investment. They are intrigued by the thoughts of preservation; they would enjoy making something out of almost nothing. Perhaps they would like to sell that "something" to someone else, or maybe just restore it and enjoy living in the renovated property with no future sale in mind.

If you plan to renovate a home solely for use as a family residence, this book will give you complete instructions on every step beyond simple redecorating, and show you how to increase the value of your property substantially. Renovators are those who are not satisfied with just "fixing up" an old home; they see renovation as a thorough and uncompromising art. However, successful ones think of themselves not only as artists but also as founders of a potentially profitable business venture—thought through in a logical and realistic manner. A renovation venture may begin and end with one house, or it may burgeon into an ongoing enterprise. In either case, the groundwork laid in the first endeavor is crucial.

If you are an investor, never forget even for a moment during the several-months-long renovation process that you are in business, that you will not stay in business long if you do not make a profit. This approach is not a callous one nor does it undercut the intrinsic satisfaction in what you are doing. Even personal pride and community esteem, though well-deserved bonuses, do not pay bills and cannot be deposited in the bank. A well-planned and business-oriented renovation can net you both a treasure of a house and treasure in your bank account.

Why the sudden upsurge of interest in older homes and buildings? Is this a fad? Statistics tell us the dramatic increase in the sales and restorations of historic and other properties is more than a passing craze. It is a trend and an economically inspired reality. Many individuals are attracted by the lower price tags on run-down but saveable relics. Now it has been proven that the margin of potential profit on a well-renovated property in a stable area is substantial.

Why? Because home-buyers are taking longer and more serious looks at older houses. They like the spaciousness, the style, and the solidarity not often found in comparably priced, new construction. Gasoline prices have forced more buyers to look for houses closer to schools, shopping or other commercial districts, thus bringing them to the inner city, towns and villages where older residences normally outnumber new ones. Sometimes, too, sellers of older homes are willing to provide long-term financing, whereas builders of newer houses are not generally willing or able to do so. The upward movement of interest rates and the availability of long-term funding also underscore the potential advantage of an older house versus a new one. The prospects of rehabilitation, particularly in cities, is capturing the attention not only of city planners and municipal governments, it is an idea now encouraged and supported by law. In 1976 and again in 1978, the Internal Revenue Law underwent major revisions to provide tax incentives for rehabilitation and tax drawbacks on demolition of historic properties.

Finally, perhaps in everyone—even those who practice an ultramodern way of life—there is a bit of fascination with the past and a desire to cling to fragments of history.

Renovation, Restoration, Preservation

While renovation, restoration and preservation are terms often used interchangeably, it is best to become acquainted with the precise definition of each. Knowledge of the scope of

4

possibilities of each can aid you as you define your own goals. Further, your reputation—if yours is a business firm—may be affected by your choice and execution of procedures. For example, do not market a house as "restored" if you have, in fact, only preserved the basics. In some cases, the difference between renovation and restoration can be significant; for instance, if you wish to apply for a grant or for special funds like those available under the National Historic Preservation Act of 1966. Further, qualification for tax incentives also requires you to make improvements in accordance with specific guidelines and standards of rehabilitation.

In *Guidelines For Rehabilitating Old Buildings* (November 1977), the U.S. Department of Housing and Urban Development and the U.S. Department of the Interior define these three words:

Renovation. The process of returning a property to a state of utility, through repair or alteration, which makes possible an efficient contemporary use. In renovation, those portions of the property important in illustrating historic, architectural, and cultural values are present. Renovation and rehabilitation are synonymous.

Restoration. The process of recovering accurately the form and details of a property as it appeared at a particular period of time by removing more modern work and by replacing missing original work.

Preservation. The process of sustaining the form and extent of a structure essentially as it now exists. Preservation aims at halting further deterioration and providing structural stability but does not contemplate significant rebuilding.

In renovated houses, some of which are illustrated here, the renovative/adaptive approach has been used.This means that in some instances a significant feature, perhaps in a kitchen or a bathroom, has been discarded in the interest of providing a completely modern and, thus, more marketable arrangement. For example, finding a claw-footed bathtub deteriorated beyond use, it might be decided to remodel, using an up-to-date enclosed tub and shower combination. Or, a kitchen may be modernized completely, retaining none of its original features but decorated in a mode consistent with the rest of the house. It has been found that many buyers want the best of both worlds.

As a beginning renovator, you will want to decide at the outset which approach works best for you and for the property you are obtaining. You do not want to find when the project is half completed that you wish you were restoring instead of renovating.

Renovation is frustrating, tedious, but personally rewarding. It is truly a "first-things-first" proposition. Often, the first tasks to be completed are the least glamorous. Wiring and plumbing, to cite two, are all but hidden from view but must be upgraded before you can move on to hanging lighting fixtures and wallpapering. Furnaces are never aesthetic delights, yet they are essential, especially if you expect contractors and other workmen to stay on the job more than fifteen minutes in the winter. The list goes on and on.

Using this book as your tool, you can plan your renovation so that it is orderly, progresses without major setbacks and delays, and will ultimately reflect quality workmanship.

Emotions ride on the surface of a renovation-undertaking. It is often difficult for renovators to be able to separate themselves emotionally from their property long enough to make wise decisions. As the building or the home begins to assume its own character and charm, renovators need to step back and look at it through the eyes of the marketplace rather than in terms of their own specific preferences. Though you may love carpeting, you must sense and remember that many buyers prefer natural wood floors. If you are renovating for resale, you must be willing to defer to the market and make decisions about your "baby" that are not always consistent with your personal tastes. Also, you must be willing to "let go." It will be difficult to say good-bye to a home in which you have been working, perhaps living in, where every surface and crevice reflect an investment of your time, care, and sweat. Yet, you are in business, and that business is to renovate for a profitable resale. Let these thoughts serve as a daily reminder.

As for business renovation—when is the best time to begin a renovation business? Any time, if you are cautious and thorough in defining your goals, in building confidence and expertise in the marketplace and its workings, and in establishing a sound financial base from which to begin. At the outset, it is important to be conservative—perhaps even reactionary—and exercise caution by starting small. Decide what you can afford, both in terms of time and money; then, perhaps, take on a little less than that. Renovation is not a get-rich-quick scheme but if it is begun on a realistic scale, one tailored to your own abilities and capital, it can lead to a secure, ongoing and profitable venture in the end.

In renovation, you have a chance to become your own general contractor, supervising both the progress of daily tasks on the site and your own career or personal investment. The opportunities are as varied as the newel posts you will polish. The future is just as alluring as the past.

2 What To Buy ?

The Search

When you reach this point, it would be difficult to spotlight one stage in the renovation process and say, "This is the single most important decision you will make." Each step along the way calls for decisions which can and will affect your ultimate profit. But it is certainly fair to say that the selection of property is among the most crucial judgments you will make, and because it is the first big move in your career, it will shape the final outcome of your investment venture. A wise purchase will not insure your success, but a poor one can be crippling.

You might begin by being a sightseer for a while. Become a "Want Ad" reader. Peruse the lists of homes for sale and drive out to see those that appeal to you. Familiarize yourself with neighborhoods, market conditions, and areas which appear to be attractive prospects for renovation. Do some soul-searching to form a clear picture of your own motives and of your financial capabilities. Then, when you feel that you are ready to become serious, ask yourself these things:

What type of structure am I interested in buying?

How sound is my knowledge of location and my sense of the prevailing real estate market?

What are my renovation plans and goals?

How can I readily procure the assistance of a reputable, proficient realtor or real estate agent?

Have I read every page in this book? Do I remember that essential to the purchase of any property is a sound appraisal of the extent of renovation required and a total concept of the restoration business?

Type Of House

Buying a home to be used as your own personal residence is simpler than purchasing a house for renovation and quick resale. In the first case, you select a house to meet your own family's size and needs, and its location will be tailored to your individual preference. While the guidelines for the purchase and renovation of either situation would be similar, the selection of your own private home will be made to please you alone.

But suppose and assume here that your motive is renovation and resale. **You are in business** and are looking for a house, the most marketable to the greatest number of people and one which will bring the largest margin of profit when sold.

Consider what types of residences appeal to certain buyers. A spacious seven-bedroom, four-bathroom Victorian is ideal for a large family or even for a small family that has a multitude of visiting relatives and friends or happens to want a lot of space. That type will likely bring a handsome profit when sold. Now, you must consider how many such families you can expect to be clamoring for a large Victorian. In most areas, the market for this style house is rather limited, though in your own locale, you may find numerous individuals who have the desire and the cash for a rambling Victorian mansion. If such a market is there, the investment will prove wise, providing your renovation budget is not overwhelmed by all those rooms.

Much the same principle applies in reverse when considering a smaller two-bedroom, one-bathroom house. This kind is perfect for a couple, a widow, a widower, or a single individual. But again, the market may be slim and the resale could lag. Remember, when the renovation project has been completed, you must still service your debt and pay the taxes and insurance until its sale. Delays can be costly but might well be offset by the advantages of starting small with your first venture. Your initial investment will be less; your renovation costs lower. You may regard a little less profit a match for peace of mind.

There are, of course, no guarantees that your project will be profitable, but if you want to tip the scales a bit more in your favor, the best bet is to purchase a house which will hold more appeal for the majority of prospective home buyers. Most families today want at least three bedrooms, two baths, a living room, a dining room, a family room (preferably with a fireplace), a spacious kitchen, a laundry area, an adequate lot size and, depending upon the climate, a garage or carport. This style of home will, nearly always, attract more viewers, more bidders, and more buyers, even though they are impressed with the grace and the charm of a larger, old home or a quaint, small one. The faster you can sell, the less your hard-won profit will be chipped away by carrying costs and the sooner you can begin shopping for your next structure to renovate.

Type Of Location

Residential

Selecting the best location for your renovation project goes along with choosing the house itself. At the outset you are looking for a bargain and after its renovation you want to be so situated that the market will support your new, higher sales price. Before you buy, you must become well acquainted with the area in which you will be working; know something about the neighborhood's past, and have a fair idea of its future.

There are neighborhoods in the process of decline. This simply means that for some reason—deterioration of homes or schools, failure of businesses, etc.—houses are not bringing top-dollar at resale. In a less desirable area of this sort, you will probably find a bargain initially, but will your renovation create a property that is overpriced in its surroundings? If so, you may have difficulty selling or be forced to sell for a lower profit or at a loss.

True, there are many success stories of adventurous renovators who have acquired homes in declining areas, convinced friends and associates to do the same, and gradually restored the entire neighborhood. Should you have the courage and the support to attempt this kind of venture, you are to be commended. If you are a novice in the business, be aware of the great risks involved here. Make sure your collaborators are reliable and sincere before you step out on the limb!

Buying houses in neighborhoods which are changing from residential to commercial can also prove to be disadvantageous if your intended market is a residential one. However, you may open the door to an entirely new market and sell your renovated structure to professionals[1] for use as office space. Generally, ex-

[1]On two occasions, the authors sold such houses for professional use.

perience has shown, though, that the safest and most predictable investment will be within a residential area. There are simply more buyers there and your resale will come sooner.

If you have decided to invest in an area which appears to be changing, be sure to examine the applicable zoning regulations. Zoning and building-code information can be obtained through the municipal government where the property is located. Wading through code books is far from lively reading, but it is imperative that you educate yourself in these matters. If you need help, call the office of the Building Commissioner.

Finally, there are neighborhoods on the rise. Improvements are being made; the quality of the area is on the upward swing. If you can jump early into such a market, you can get a good buy and, later, profit from both your renovation and the price escalation within the environs.

While examining a certain area, review the pattern of sales for the previous few years. Prices may have increased because of inflation, but how dramatic were these increases? How do they compare with other areas in the city or town you are considering? Are homes selling quickly, or do they have aged **For Sale** signs in the yards?

What about the schools? Is the quality of education above average? Are the schools embroiled in controversy over a referendum or budget funding? Are shopping and transportation adequate? Are such municipal services as fire and police protection satisfactory? Ask all the things you would like to know if you were buying the home for your own family. In short, the least risky prospect is a neglected house in a good, stable (or rising) neighborhood with fine schools and convenient transportation and shopping nearby.

Type Of Location

Commercial

In the foregoing paragraphs, the necessity was mentioned of familiarizing yourself with commercial and residential zoning regulations. Should you decide to purchase property for commercial use, be prepared to do some additional homework so that you will understand the nature of this complex market. Seek aid from a realtor or a real estate agent who specializes in commercial property. In most metropolitan areas, the best commercial real estate specialists are to be found in commercial real estate firms. While there are many residential real estate firms that are developing commercial divisions, these firms are not likely to be as experienced as those dealing exclusively in commercial properties.

Looking into the renovation of commercial structures, you will discover that these sites generally carry much higher price tags than do residential. Financing will be more difficult to obtain. Your market will be limited, not only because it is commercial but also because fewer businesses will opt for charm and style over the convenience of a modern structure.

A first venture is, therefore, suggested in residential rather than in commercial property. Then, if your residential undertaking is successful, you may feel equipped to experiment in the commercial arena. Do proceed, though, on a limited scale. Remember that a move from a $50,000 residential renovation to a $200,000 commercial one requires a quantum leap in capital, expenditures, and expertise. Be sure you are ready.

Your Renovation Goals

In Chapter One, the terms renovation, restoration, and preservation were defined. Because you are in search of profit, you are probably thinking either renovation or restoration. As you inspect properties, begin to formulate your plans; decide whether you will renovate or restore. If the property is recognized by the Historic or Landmarks Commission in your area, there may be restrictions on what can and cannot be done to the exterior. Adapt your goals accordingly.

In most cases where the renovative/adaptive approach is used, this means that the attempt is made to restore all style elements of the property that will lend to its aesthetic and historic appeal. It should be kept in mind, however, that despite the architectural significance, most prospective buyers are seeking a structure tailored to the needs of modern living. Bathrooms and kitchens and all other parts of the home must be updated.

The Seizure

(Pounding the pavement)

The more complete your exposure in the marketplace, the better your chances of zeroing in on the perfect renovation prospect.

1. Continue to watch the classified ads in your local newspaper. Follow up on those which seem to meet your specifications.

2. Advise your realtor or real estate agent of the precise nature of your needs.

3. Drive around, look for older, abandoned houses. If you find one that appeals to you, do not be deterred by the mere absence of a **For Sale** sign! Check with the people around the house to learn the owner's name. If they do not know, do some research at the deed office of the courthouse. Then get in touch with the owner and ask if the house is for sale. If so, make an offer. If not, give him your name, address, and telephone number, requesting him/her to contact you if he decides to sell at a later date.

4. Place a classified ad in your local newspaper: **Want to buy older home to renovate, prefer three or four bedrooms in the . . . area.**

5. If you have a Historic or Landmarks Commission, let it know of your interest in renovating an older house; attend its meetings.

6. If you spy an occupied house you like, take the direct approach. Knock on the door, introduce yourself, explain that you have been admiring the house and would like very much to make

an offer on it if he/she wishes to sell it. Leave your name, address, and telephone number should he express an interest in maybe selling at a later time. Intrepid renovators make this technique a practice, marching from door to door of homes that look promising. The renovators gain exposure (notoriety even) and, should an owner decide to sell, all parties benefit through these prior contacts.

Relocating Houses

("Thanks! I'll take it with me!")

Buying a desirable house situated in an unpleasing location or in an area that is to be cleared, and moving it to a more suitable location is an alternative that has merit. You get more house for less money; then simply move it to a place where it will command a premium when sold.

Simple? Not really, but certainly possible. This method does require an extra step or two. You must, of course, move the house; you must acquire its future site. You are not able to just "park it" until you come upon the perfect site for its relocation.

The finding of a desirable, new site for a movable house should be governed by the identical rules for selecting developed property. You must consider the price you pay for the lot in your overall estimation of profitability. Next, determine whether the house you have selected is, in fact, movable. You will want to check into all regulations in the community in reference to home relocation. There will be height, width, and size restrictions. Obtain clearance on all "required permits" before entering your bid. Assistance with these problems will come as you begin talking to house-moving companies and compiling their estimates and listening to their opinions. Many thorough estimates should precede any bid to purchase the home. Do not delay, however; someone else may act before you do.

The cost of moving a house varies with its size, distance to be moved, number of power lines which have to be dropped, and the section of the country in which the move is to take place. Very roughly speaking, an average 1,500-square-foot, one-story, frame house can be moved for from $3,000-$5,000; a two-story, frame for $5,000-$7,000; while a brick residence adds from $2,000-$4,000 to those base figures. In addition, there is the cost of the new lot which may range anywhere from $5,000-$20,000 or more, depending upon size, neighborhood, and market value. To these, add the $2,000-$4,000 price of preparing a foundation at the new site. The figure for moving an eight-room, brick house could run as high as $11,000 for moving, $10,000 for the lot, and $4,000 for site preparation, for a conservative total of $25,000. If the price of a comparable house in a preferential area is higher, then the relocation is worth pursuing.

Sometimes there are houses that are literally given away to save demolition costs when the land is to be cleared for commercial building, highway construction, or parking lots. To render the transaction legal, it may cost you only a token fee of $10-$25. Even if the owner does not give the house away, excellent prospects can be found for $100-$1,000. Homes marked for demolition are frequently diamonds in the rough, featuring the superb craftsmanship and quality materials of yesteryear. Here, too, relocation may be feasible and will often cost less than buying a house and renovating it in its original location.

How can such houses be found?

1. Write a letter to the right-of-way engineer of your State Department of Highways and Transportation and ask that your name be placed on its mailing list to receive notification of any house in your area being placed on public auction.

2. Get in touch with moving companies and demolition firms who may have information on houses scheduled to be demolished.

3. Watch the newspaper for articles about new highway construction, then look for advertisements of the houses that must be sold and removed from the right-of-way.

4. Note newspaper stories of such large-scale construction projects as airports, stadia, parks, civic auditoriums, lakes, reservoirs and malls; survey those places to see if there is a house worth moving.

5. Colleges and universities are good source-areas of old homes that have outlived their institutional usefulness and must be moved or razed for construction of dormitory or classroom facilities. Call the college construction engineers and explain your interest in old houses scheduled for demolition or removal.

6. Watch for zoning hearings involving residential property being rezoned as commercial. You may find a house you like in the newly rezoned area; if so, learn the name of the owner and offer a price based on your promise to remove the structure from its site.

7. Communicate with your local Historic or Landmarks Commission, expressing your desire to buy, renovate and, if necessary, move an endangered historic house.

The most discouraging aspect of buying and moving a house is that the larger, older houses, the best built and least expensive to obtain, are often the most difficult to move. Normally, they cannot be moved very far because of various legal restrictions. If a moving permit is procured, you may find that a large house does not travel well; for one thing, it tends to clip telephone and power lines as it goes by (the mere cost of dropping or replacing these lines can make the move prohibitive). In addition, the roof and porches frequently must be removed in order to meet height and width requirements and their replacement costs run up the price of renovation.

When you heap together all the complications in relocating a house, you may be inclined to dismiss this idea as out-of-hand. Do not. Think of it as a creative, worthwhile alternative, one which can increase profits to the extra-innovative renovator.

Commercial/Industrial Properties *versus* Residential

Generally, residential properties are faster-moving resales than either commercial or industrial ones. There are more people purchasing houses than there are businesses buying commercial or industrial properties. Also, commercial/industrial properties have higher price tags, and obtaining financing is more difficult and complex. The market is totally different between commercial/industrial and residential. Once you have mastered the residential market, you may or may not desire to go into the other field.

Following your profitable undertaking in the residential field (again whether as an individual, or on an investment or company basis), you should then consider, following detailed analysis, whether you want to venture into the commercial/industrial area. As a word of caution, you probably will be more successful dealing in the $30,000-$60,000 residential market. If you enter into a commercial/industrial property-purchase for several hundred thousand dollars, however, and are not successful, you may be totally out of business unless you have substantial financial strength to tide you over.

Renovating Property For Rental Income

Rental property can be extremely time-consuming and may not be very rewarding financially unless you have a sufficient number of units to allow you the employment of maintenance personnel. Should you purchase for rental a single-family home, a duplex, a quadriplex, or a small apartment, be absolutely certain that these properties are close to your residence or to your business so that you will have adequate time to take care of defective plumbing, wiring, roof work, burned-out light bulbs, stuck windows, scraped walls, and other details which can become overwhelming in your daily schedule. On another positive note, rental property may be renovated for resale or, if you maintain ownership, can afford significant tax benefits.

The best recommendation, again, is to begin with the renovation/restoration of single-family structures, then expand afterward into other real estate prospects, if you so desire. Spreading your or your company's assets too thin at the beginning can be disastrous. You should endeavor to conquer, one step at a time, and not cover all the bases on "day one."

3 Bidding: The Bottom Line

When it comes to bidding, acquiring a house for the sole purpose of profitable renovation is vastly different from buying a home for a personal residence. The purchaser, in determining a fair offer on a home-to-be, considers the prevailing value of comparable houses in the area, the size of the mortgage and monthly payments, and the cost of improvements to be made over a long period.

In seeking a house for renovation and resale, the purchaser is in somewhat of a vacuum. If it is a real derelict, there may be none in the area to which it can be compared. Besides, the investor/renovator hopes to make major alterations in a shorter time and, because he/she is planning for a speedy resale, there will be no help from the curse of inflation (typically a key factor in real estate appreciation).

Recall that the seller may have been operating in the same vacuum when he determined the listing price, so forget the asking-price and work with your own.

1. Begin by evaluating the property as it will be **after** renovation. Compare with other well-kept homes in the area to see what your house might bring when completed.

2. Know the general market in the area where the house is located. In other words, do not plan a renovation that will result in a structure that outprices the neighborhood. If the average house is in the $50,000 range, you could have trouble selling a renovated one that has blossomed to $100,000.

3. Determine renovation expenditures. (A checklist for this purpose has been printed at the end of this section).

4. Estimate length of time necessary for renovation. Do not be overly optimistic. In reality, be super-conservative, allowing for every possible contingency from plumbers' strikes to major floods.

5. Determine what amount of profit you wish to derive after all costs have been accounted for. Take into consideration the value of your own time invested in this project, as opposed to other money-making ventures.

6. When you begin the actual calculations that will result in your offer, **do not** start with the listing price and work forward; rather, begin with the estimated resale price and work backwards. Your formula (simplified) will look like this: resale price after renovation minus renovation costs minus any commissions and closing costs minus profit margin, equals fair price to pay.

If you come up with a figure far lower than the owners are asking, either the house is overpriced, or it is not for you. You still have two options: come in with a firm bid at your price, or take a pass altogether.

Bidding on a house is an emotional experience, even for those determined to remain aloof. By the time you are ready to bid, you will have seen the residence several times, have begun to identify with it, have fallen in love with its charming little eccentricities, and have seen marvelous potential in every room. There may be other buyers also clamoring for the house. The more you think about it, the more difficult it is to let go. In fact, you may be prone to edge your bid a little higher than is practical.

Do not fail to remember that you are in this for profit. Each time you hedge, you take a little edge from the potential gain. It is possible to sneak your way right into a no-win situation before you have even begun.[2]

A word about counter-offers. They are customary bargaining tools the seller uses to answer your bid with another price — lower than his first listing, but higher than your bid. Many buyers adjust their first offer slightly lower than the price they would be willing to pay, allowing for the probability that the seller will counter. Others make their first offer their firm and only one. This is an unadvisable practice. Make an offer lower than the price you are really willing to pay because, generally, most everyone likes to bargain. Both the buyer and the seller then can return with as many counter-offers as they wish and may spend days tossing figures back and forth until a selling price will have been established. It pays to take a good look at any reasonable counter-offer. Sometimes, the buyer and the seller split the difference; that is, if the buyer's first offer was $20,000 and the seller's counter was $25,000, the final price might be established at $22,500. Both parties feel they have completed a good **deal:** the buyer has purchased below the listed price, and the seller has enticed the buyer to a slightly higher dollar amount.

[2]The authors have bid on a number of houses; have passed on many; and have also let go numerous counter-offers from sellers which would have taken them above their projected figures. Probably, only one out of every twenty homes on which they bid was actually purchased.

Renovation Costs: The Big "If"

How do you arrive at the estimated cost of your renovation? The answer is, laboriously. While this section precedes information on the renovation project (Chapters 8-13) itself, it is wise to be completely familiar with that material before evaluating any property. At the end of this chapter is a checklist quite helpful in projecting costs.

You may need to add other cost-categories pertinent to a particular structure. Some listed here may not be applicable. The list looks overwhelming and causes one to wonder, "How do you make all of the estimates thoroughly, yet quickly enough to beat your competition?"

1. As you examine each room, make a detailed list of what needs to be done. Consider replacement items, repairs and decorating.

2. Obtain prices on supplies, appliances and fixtures from dealers or building contractors. (In most instances, you will pay wholesale or contractors' prices for materials bought).

3. Arrange for contractors to come to the premises for estimates on work and services to be performed (Chapter 10). You will need the cooperation of the seller and/or the real estate agent for this. However, the least inconvenience to the seller's schedule is recommended.

4. Many estimates can be handled by telephone if you can provide exact specifications, i.e., size of surfaces (for paint, wallpaper, carpet, floor refinishing, tile, etc.). While viewing the house, make these and other measurements you might need for your cost inquiries.

5. If there is not enough time to arrive at careful, ballpark figures, or if the seller is uncooperative, drop out. It is not worth the risk to guess.

6. A seller may be willing to accept a contract from you, contingent upon the completion of the necessary estimates. If there is stiff competition for the property, this is unlikely, but it is a possible avenue to explore, nonetheless.

7. If you are a first-time renovator, avoid letting time-pressures push you into a hasty decision. The time will come when you will have the experience and the resources to make sound estimates on your own without having to consult each sub-contractor on every single job.

RENOVATION ESTIMATE CHECK-LIST

You may think of additional cost-categories that need to be considered. These major ones will help to provide you with the basis for a final decision:

1. Cost of structure $ _____
2. Cost of moving (optional) $ _____
3. Cost of lot (optional) $ _____
4. Legal fees and closing costs on purchase $ _____
5. Clean-up (labor and supplies) $ _____
6. Roof $ _____
7. Structural repairs/siding $ _____
8. Gutters $ _____
9. Exterior painting
   Labor $ _____
   Supplies $ _____
10. Interior painting
    Labor $ _____
    Supplies $ _____
11. Wallpaper
    Labor $ _____
    Supplies $ _____
12. Heating system/repairs or replacement $ _____
13. Air conditioning/repairs or replacement, or installation $ _____
14. Plumbing $ _____
15. Wiring $ _____
16. Termite inspection/correction $ _____
17. Landscaping
    Labor $ _____
    Seeds, plants/gardening materials $ _____
18. Pre-renovation clean-up $ _____
19. Post-renovation clean-up $ _____
20. Floors $ _____
21. Carpeting $ _____
22. Kitchen
    Labor $ _____
    Supplies/materials $ _____
    Cooking unit/repairs or replacement $ _____
    Dishwasher/repairs or replacement $ _____
    Refrigerator/repairs or replacement $ _____

23. Bathroom 1
    Labor $ _____
    Supplies/materials $ _____
    Bathroom 2
    Labor $ _____
    Supplies/materials $ _____
    Miscellaneous bathroom fixtures $ _____
24. Windows $ _____
25. Fireplaces and mantels $ _____
26. Basement $ _____
27. Attic $ _____
28. Vaulted-roof ceiling $ _____
29. Additions to structure $ _____
30. Porches/piazzas $ _____
31. Insulation $ _____
32. Laundry Room $ _____
33. Miscellaneous $ _____
34. Insurance $ _____
35. Sign: For Sale By Owner $ _____
36. Advertising $ _____
37. Carpentry (trim work and repair) $ _____
38. Sheetrock or plaster repair/replace $ _____
39. Light fixtures (exterior/interior) $ _____
40. Door hardware, switch plates $ _____
41. Driveways (repair/replace) $ _____
42. Permits (where applicable) $ _____
43. Real estate commission $ _____
44. Closing/legal expenses—on sale $ _____

                                  TOTAL $ _____

The Purchase

Contracts, Closings Statements and Legal Counsel

4

Unless your own background includes legal or real estate training, you will probably reach certain junctures along the renovation route that will require you to seek professional advice. This does not mean that you need to consult an attorney every time documents or happenings become a bit complicated. There are some mazes a renovator can get through alone; however, others require professional guidance. An attorney can provide the degree of legal assistance required, with the amount to be paid for such services depending on those rendered, gauged in most cases by the client. How much do you want to depend on your attorney?

A to Z legal advice is recommended highly for your first foray. Be sure not to become overconfident by increased legal exposure and adopt the do-it-yourself attitude.

Your contracts should be drawn properly, either from a buying or a selling viewpoint. Otherwise, you could possibly lose an amount greatly in excess of the aggregate legal fees that you might pay over several years. For instance, this can occur in just one transaction if there should be a defective title. To cite, you may have purchased a house for $20,000, spent $15,000 in renovating, and then offered to sell for $50,000, to yield a very profitable, potential return. If you should then discover that the title is defective, that someone else has a bona fide claim to the land, including the residence, you could lose your total investment of $35,000, plus your potential profit of $15,000, in addition to all of the other expenses you probably would incur trying to retain the property. Less extreme, but still costly, would be a situation in which, following renovation, a roofer appears with an unpaid bill for a roof installed by the previous owner. A title search at the time of your purchase should have indicated the unpaid lien, thus avoiding the surprise liability. Your attorney can provide a title **opinion**, generally supported by "professional errors and omissions insurance," or advise that you purchase a formal Title Insurance Policy which gives increased protection from a loss. Depending upon the circumstances, there may be other such specific legal obstacles as zoning requirements, code regulations or parking variances. Both the novice and the experienced purchaser are well-advised to utilize the services of an attorney in these and other complex situations. Perhaps your real estate agent can shed additional light on certain of the issues as well.

Lawyers are, for the greatest number, bonded on their opinions, and it is recommended that you select a well-respected legal firm experienced in real estate. As you would not seek an orthopedic surgeon for a coronary condition, you would not employ an attorney who was not fully informed on real estate matters. Real estate is a specialized field in the business community and can be very complex. If you have the right attorney, the services will be well worth the effort and fees. Some purchases or sales often end up in emotional conflict over circumstances neither anticipated, pleasant nor important. A top-flight attorney is essential in some cases to appease a tense situation and settle a matter logically, legally, and to your benefit.

Following are useful guidelines, whether you are buying or selling a property:

I. Buying Property
    A.   Contract of Sale
        1.   Know what you are buying. Make sure that the property is legally and properly described in the contract. (Most property is sold in an "as is" condition). Anything extra—such as work or repairs to be done by the seller at his expense—should be in writing. Make certain any agreement you may have with the seller is in writing, as a part of the contract.

        2.   Be positive that the contract specifies that the seller must convey to you at closing time a title-insurable deed or similar document approved by your attorney. Whether or not you should buy title insurance depends upon your lawyer's advice and, ultimately, upon your decision.

        3.   If dealing with a real estate agent, require him/her to give you a "net sheet" well in advance of the closing date. This should include all of your costs and specify the exact, total expenses relating to the transaction, and how much money you will need at closing.

        4.   Finally, be positive that you have an enforceable contract. It might be well to add the wording, "If purchaser has to sue for specific performance of this contract, the seller will pay all costs of the action, including reasonable attorney's fees." You may decide to have your lawyer review the final documents before you sign.

    B.   Before closing
        1.   Have the title checked by your lawyer for ownership records (a person cannot convey a piece of property he doesn't own), liens, current taxes due, etc.

        2.   Check to see if all water, electricity, gas and sewer bills (if applicable) have been paid by the seller and are current as of the closing date. If not, make sure they are taken out of the seller's proceeds at closing and paid immediately. Have these and other accounts (if any) put into the purchaser's name as of closing date.

        3.   Obtain necessary and proper insurance coverage (Chapter 6) and have binder or policy available at closing.

        4.   See that all contingency items that may have been in the contract (i.e., seller was to do certain work on property, etc., before closing) are satisfied.

The nature of the closing statement involving your purchase or sale will depend upon the specific circumstances of the transaction. In some states, the real estate broker is authorized to prepare closing statements, whereas in other areas, an attorney or legal representative of the lending institution is required. If someone other than an attorney is authorized and qualified to perform this task, you may be wise to bypass the attorney for this service, thereby saving the fees you would have paid and using these funds for more pressing matters like a title search.

II. Selling Property
    A. Contract of Sale
        1. It is a good idea to include the clause "Property is being sold in 'as is' condition, with the following stipulations . . ." This allows both the seller and the purchaser to provide for any contingencies with a clear understanding of exactly what is being bought and what is being sold.

        2. Be sure to specify which closing costs are to be paid by the seller and which by the purchaser.

        3. Add the clause, "If any provisions of this contract are held to be not enforceable, then the remaining provisions will stay in full force and effect." This may keep some small, insignificant, unenforceable provision from voiding an otherwise sound contract.

        4. As in a **Contract to Purchase**, have your real estate agent, if any, prepare a "net sheet" well in advance of closing.

        5. When you, as seller, accept a contract, it should, obviously, have a closing date. Just as important is an acceptance date, i.e., the date the purchaser must notify you that all contingencies, such as financing, have been met and that he will be able to close the transaction as agreed. This is particularly important in order that your property will not be tied up for a lengthy time on the gamble that the property's purchaser will be able to obtain proper financing. Remember, the signing of a contract by buyer and seller does not always mean that the property is sold.

    B. Before Closing
        1. Cut off or transfer all water, sewer and power services as of date of closing.

        2. Cancel your insurance policy as of date of closing.

In review, you are well advised to know your facts before you consult an attorney, whether on a property closing or any complex legal problem. Learn as much as you can on your own about the situation under consideration and draw up a list of specific questions or concerns. While other points may arise throughout your consultation, a thorough grasp of the topic will expedite communication. Most lawyers bill by the hour, and excellent ones usually charge steep fees. Remember that the meter starts ticking when you say "howdy." The better prepared you are, the sooner you can say "thank you," and turn the meter to the **off** position.

5 In Search Of Financing

Long before you decide to renovate—whether as a family enterprise or as a burgeoning small business—you will, no doubt, have given more than a passing thought to how you will finance your project.

You should have a vise-like grip on the state of your own finances, and know precisely the limit of the amount of the mortgage or loan you can assume, and have a reasonable idea of what amount of funds you will be able to borrow to finance the renovation. You should know how much you can afford on a monthly basis to service your debt and still buy groceries. Also, become aware of the various types of financing that are available for the purposes you have in mind.

You will need more than a vision to qualify for a loan. Before you approach a financial institution, you will need to have a file filled with facts and at least one pocket full of assets.

How can you do this? Assume you are entering the renovation business as an individual on a first-time try. You do not have bundles of ready cash but you do have enough assets to make a down-payment. Moreover, you have an eye toward a permanent career in the renovation business and you want to be classified by the financial institution you approach as a person specializing in house renovation, not as a real estate speculator. Your best method, then, is one combining professionalism with a thorough knowledge of mortgage and home-improvement financing.

The Conventional Mortgage

In securing a conventional mortgage, most lending institutions make available 75 to 80 percent loans on the price you are paying for the house, conditioned upon a qualified appraisal and a satisfactory credit history. (There are also other programs that provide up to 95 percent financing in some cases). No matter what the percentage, the remainder (down payment) is derived by the buyer through "internal financing," which means simply your own cash savings, income, salary, or from the sale of stocks, bonds, land, buildings or other assets.

The important point to remember when considering a conventional mortgage is that in a very real sense it is an installment "purchase." You must meet monthly payments that may include funds for escrow deposits such as insurance and real estate taxes. Because you are in the renovation business, you must make sure these payments do not excessively deplete your cash reserve, resulting in your having little left over for the project itself.

It is wise, when you begin your house shopping, to have a handy book of mortgage tables, which can be obtained from a financial institution. In it you will find charts that will show you the exact monthly payments required at a given interest rate for an exact-size mortgage loan. To this figure add real estate taxes (most lenders require approximately one-twelfth of the estimated yearly taxes with each monthly payment) and insurance (using the same one-twelfth rule). If no escrow account is required, your monthly payment will be the one found in the mortgage tables, but be sure you save enough for taxes and insurance payments.

Assurance of your ability to meet your monthly obligations is particularly critical if you plan to continue in business. Late payments will do little to enhance your professional status when the time comes to buy house number two.

Conventional Mortgage Plus Renovation Funding

At the time you are seeking mortgage financing, you must also be sure that sufficient renovation funds will be available. The avenue most likely to open through the conventional mortgage route is a Rehabilitation Loan. This is not to be confused with a Home Improvement Loan, obtained for such specific purposes as remodeling a kitchen, adding a new roof, or paving a driveway.

A Rehabilitation Loan is more closely related to a Construction Loan, and is used to fund an entire project.

It is often set up this way: the lender pledges a certain amount of funds at a given interest rate and the borrower pays a "commitment fee." The borrower then draws against the funds as they are needed and pays interest on those used, when they are used. The borrower is normally required to provide security against these monies; the security being the house itself. Essentially, what you are doing here is borrowing against your equity in the building via property mortgage financing.

Should you apply to a commercial bank or a savings and loan institution? This decision will be based, in part, on any personal relationship you have established previously with one or the other. However, if your first renovation attempt also represents your first time to acquire a loan, experience indicates that the greatest advantage will come from a commercial bank. The reasons are twofold:

1. Since S&L credit extensions are longer and, consequently, more risky, appraisals from savings and loan institutions on houses needing renovation tend to be lower; the loan amount available may be insufficient for the purchase and you may have to dig deeper into your own savings to make up the difference. The result may be a strain on your cash reserves.

2. Even if you are able to obtain an adequate appraisal and qualify for savings and loan financing on a permanent basis, you will more likely pay higher closing costs and fees which will reduce your final profit.

At this point in your project, savings and loan financing probably constitutes the least desirable of all financing sources. Try first at commercial banks; utilize the savings and loan services only to supplement your main source of funds. A S&L prefers to make permanent loans on the finished product.

As a renovator, you may find that many lending institutions, whether they are banks or savings and loans, are not as eager to see you as their advertisements would imply. Many will be leery of lending significant sums for renovation of older, run-down residences. All may not have your quality of vision; therefore, the demands on you will be greater to do your homework painstakingly. Display a sound financial picture and present your intentions in a well-informed manner.

Commercial Loan From A Bank

Another type of financing is a direct loan obtained from a commercial bank. As a borrower for a first-time renovation, you might have difficulty securing a loan, but it **is** worth a try. This is something to keep in mind, for sure, as your reputation grows and you establish a good working relationship with the financial community.

Here is how a commercial bank loan works: the bank makes a commitment to the borrower for a given amount of funds on an interim basis (the typical time period is one year), the size of the commitment being based on the financial strength of the borrower and the value of the property. The loan can be set up in two ways:

1. Unsecured. Of course, this type is the most desirable since no collateral is required. It is fast, eliminating the delay that often results when collateral is pledged. A quick financial decision is to your advantage as time is often critical when purchasing property. If you are a new customer, though, an unsecured loan may be hard to obtain.

As your reputation and your association with a particular banking institution grow, the bank may be willing to establish an unsecured line of credit for you. Here, the bank commits a certain sum and the borrower draws upon it as needed. Such credit adds to your financial flexibility; you can now make an immediate offer on a desirable piece of property without having to wait for a loan decision or an appraisal. Being able to complete a transaction promptly can win you a "buy" at a lower price than might have been possible had you been forced to negotiate while waiting for financial arrangements to be made. Also, a delay awaiting a bank appraisal or approval can result in the seller changing his mind, deciding to "up" the price, or conveying the property to someone else. If possible, "have" and "use" this line of credit, so that valuable property can be bought quickly with the readily available funds.

2. Secured. In this case, the borrower secures the loan by

pledging collateral from such outside sources as stocks, bonds, securities, or the equity owned in property other than that for which the loan is sought. It is important to be aware that commercial banks can make unsecured loans. Savings and loan institutions are not permitted to do so.

Mortgage From The Seller

Obtaining a mortgage from the seller constitutes a superb financial technique, especially in a case of renovation for profit. If you intend to sell the property immediately after renovation, your need for funds is short-term. If the seller should not need or desire all of the proceeds at the time of closing, you may be able to make a mortgage arrangement with him. In times of high interest rates and a shortage of funds from financial institutions, owner financing is critical to buyer and seller alike.

Under this method, the seller obtains a note and mortgage from you and you pay principal and interest, or just interest. The payments can be set up monthly, quarterly, or yearly. The property is the collateral. The amount of the loan, the period it covers, and the interest rate are points negotiated between the seller and the buyer. There are advantages to be gained by both parties:

FOR THE SELLER

1. In times of "tight money" (unavailability of money through standard means), this is an excellent way for a seller to make his property more desirable for sale.

2. The interest rate you will pay him will most probably be higher than he can obtain through most alternative investments with the same degree of safety.

3. The mortgage can be tailored to both parties' needs.

4. The renovation will rapidly increase the value of the property which you are pledging as collateral, thus reducing seller's risk.

FOR THE BUYER

1. You can save on closing costs and loan fees.

2. You will probably secure the loan at a lower interest rate than that offered by a lending institution.

3. A seller can usually offer more flexible terms than a financial institution.

4. In times of "tight money" this may be the only means by which you can maintain your inventory of properties.

It is advisable upon entering into such an arrangement to consult an attorney and have him assist you with the terms of the loan and the usury regulations in your state.

VA/FHA Financing

Government-guaranteed loans from the VA or FHA are best utilized when financing the final product following renovation. Their terms often make the financing a real "selling" feature to prospective buyers because the down payment is generally lower and other terms are more tailored to the purchaser's benefit. Remember, however, sellers pay the "points."

As you examine your own financial status, and as you begin to decide what property you want to acquire, be sure to exercise extreme caution against overextending yourself.[3]

As a renovator, you must be imaginative. You can even be daring, but you should never be fearless.

Whether you are an investor or a potential homeowner, permanent financing is crucial to your survival unless you happen to be extremely wealthy. Even in that instance, you might desire financing as a hedge against inflation.

When you purchase and improve a property with personal savings and/or a short-term loan, always remember that either you will eventually sell to someone or will decide to keep it as an investment. In either case, the primary way is permanent long-term financing. If the funds are not available or too expensive through financial institutions or private sources, you may be locked into a corner. The clue here is to keep yourself current always on the financial times in general and real estate in particular.

---

[3]Early in the authors' business career, they experienced the pangs of overextension. They had purchased five houses, each being an excellent buy, but requiring extensive renovation. The down payments and the monthly obligations had depleted their cash reserves to the extent that one morning they discovered that their checking account balance was $57. On that day, they would have returned gladly one or two bargains to the sellers in exchange for solid footing. They were stalemated, anticipating disaster, but were lucky. One of the houses sold and their cash flow was restored. Not without a setback, however—specifically, worry.

6 Insurance: "Don't Leave Home Without It"

Whether you are renovating a house for an investment, for resale, or merely to live in, insurance coverage is highly important.

Even if you have a house that you are planning to keep only a few months, the property should be insured against fire, windstorm, vandalism and other damage. During the renovation process, a house is even more vulnerable than before you started work on it.[4] If the house you have bought has been occupied by vagrants or other homeless persons as an unofficial hotel, they likely will resent being evicted. Numerous renovators find that, after they have secured the premises by repairing doors, installing new locks, and replacing broken windows, extensive damage oc-

---

[4] The authors renovated a large, older house in an inner-city area which for years had been used as a haven for vagrants, winos and transients who were not happy about being dispossessed. The new owners asked the help of the police in clearing the area of the unwelcome inhabitants. Turned out each morning, each evening the vagrants were back. The dispersal continued for several weeks—as did the theft of tools and materials. Then one day, the owners, intrigued by these people, approached one and offered him a job during the renovation as watchman at an agreed-upon fee, allowing him to occupy the house during the renovation process. He accepted and the theft and vandalism ceased. There was one minor snag, though. The local police, unaware of his new position, upon seeing him on the premises the first night he was hired, promptly escorted the "night watchman" downtown, as the expression goes. Subsequently, all was well after his identification by the owners.

curs afterward. A former occupant will sometimes break down a door or smash a window in order to seek shelter from rain or the cold. Also, abandoned houses have sometimes become favorite meeting places for teenagers. The fact that you have bought the house does not mean that you are immune from unauthorized occupants or danger from fire or vandalism. Although insurance is expensive, it is well worth the price.

In the past, insuring an older residence has been a problem. If you have bought the place to renovate and to resell, or if you are not living in the home while renovation is going on, the house is not eligible generally for a homeowner's policy. You can obtain a fire, extended coverage, and a vandalism policy, which is more appropriate. Be cautioned, however, that this policy does not provide theft coverage, either of tools and building supplies or parts of the building itself (fixtures, doors, etc.). Here, as in other insurance matters, the counsel of a competent insurance agent should be sought.

All property-insurance policies have stipulations on how much of replacement cost may or must be carried on the building. "Replacement cost" to insurance companies does not reflect the value of the land; it centers around the reconstruction of the physical structure. For this reason, market value or purchase price is seldom more than a starting point in arriving at an insurable value. If you find that insurance companies are reluctant to insure your newly discovered "treasure," consider a substantial deductible. Some insurance companies are more attracted to an $80,000 policy with a $1,000 deductible than a $40,000 one with a $50 or $100 deductible. To be reimbursed for the cost of an entire building, you would have to insure for 100 per cent of the value. This replacement-cost formula works with new house construction, and most owners insure for close to the market or replacement value. Contrarily, an older home presents a different problem. You may have paid only $40,000 for your ten-room Victorian house, but should the property be destroyed by fire, the duplication might cost $80,000-$100,000. Replacing those wide-plank, heart-pine floors, the intricately carved paneling, the ornate gingerbread mouldings, and the lath and plaster walls is very expensive and, often, virtually impossible.

Most insurance companies are leery of insuring such a structure for $40,000, because the premium may not produce enough income to cover small but costly-to-duplicate claims. They are also reluctant to insure such a house for $80,000 or $100,000; this would be overinsuring in terms of market value. To do so would mean that the house would be worth more destroyed than "as is," and could lead to a fraudulent-claim climate.

The difficulty of obtaining insurance for older houses has been solved somewhat with new versions of homeowners' policies that have been developed to alleviate the problem.

One version of the new homeowner's policy insures the older home with the stipulation that the insurer will pay for repairing any damage occurring, provided modern construction materials are used in replacement, i.e., you must use dry wall instead of duplicating the original lath and plaster, and wall-to-wall carpeting over a plywood base rather than heart-pine floors. If the insurance company and the insured are unable to agree on appropriate substitute materials, a cash-value claim is allowed. The time for such discussions is before a building may be destroyed or severely damaged. Most reliable insurance agents will point that out, discussing with you how a loss will be settled. The insurance policy is a legal contract and will do only what it says it will.

If you are renovating the structure to be used as your residence, then the completed building will probably be eligible for a homeowner's policy, combining house, contents, liability and other coverages under one policy. There are various kinds and forms of homeowners' policies; consult your insurance agent for the coverage most suited to your particular situation.

Another homeowner's policy provides that all losses shall be paid on a cash-value basis, with the total not to exceed repair or replacement value.

Both versions revise coverage for various hazards, in some cases reducing payments, as for example, limiting compensation for any one theft up to $1,000.

These new insurance plans put the cost of insuring older residences in a more moderate premium range. The cost per $1,000 of coverage may still be more, but the total premium will be lower because older-house owners will be free to insure for **less** than replacement cost.

But the point remains that insurance coverage is one of the vitally important details to take care of when becoming involved in a renovation project. Also, do not overlook general liability and a workmen's compensation policy before you begin the project.

A few important thoughts about insurance have been included here because it is so necessary, both from a cost and a commonsense standpoint. Seek the services of a competent insurance agent.

7 Tax Tips

There can be various tax benefits—such as capital gains—related to the holding of real estate beyond a certain period of time. However, prior to your taking any particular tax advantages on your individual and/or company returns, it is recommended that you review this with your CPA, other accountant, or legal counsel. Laws and tax rulings are changing constantly on a broad basis, as are rulings pertaining to capital gains and losses. What is actually a deductible renovation-expense and what is an expense that should be depreciated varies according to a number of circumstances. As you already know from reviewing your business or personal tax return, few rulings are ironclad from year to year. In essence, "general opinions" on taxes are treacherous guidelines to follow. To comply with the current laws and to obtain the maximum deductions, knowledgeable counsel should be retained. Of course, like all other subjects, the more you are informed personally, the less you will have to rely on your tax adviser. Be informed but not overconfident.

Tax Incentives For Rehabilitation

The 1976 Internal Revenue Code is a reversal from an earlier position favoring demolition/replacement of older structures and, instead, provides incentives for the preservation of buildings having historical or architectural interest. These new laws were included in the Tax Reform Act of 1976, under section 2124, entitled, "Tax Incentives to Encourage the Preservation of Historic Structures." In general, this ruling is meant to encourage rehabilitation by allowing rapid amortization of rehabilitation costs, or accelerated depreciation of certain expenses. In addition, investment tax credit can provide valuable benefits.

Properties which could be affected by the new law include such historic commercial structures as office buildings, stores, theatres, apartment buildings, warehouses, factories, and other properties used for the production of income, including rental homes.

In order to qualify for tax incentives, a project must be designated as a "certified rehabilitation" of a "certified historic structure." A certified historic structure is listed in *The National Register of Historic Places*, is located in a *National Register* Historic District and certified by the Secretary of the Interior as being significant to that district, or stands in a historic district designated under a state or local statute. A certified rehabilitation is one approved by the Secretary of the Interior.

A rather disarming capsule, is it not? Not if you take the process one step at a time. If you feel your property may qualify, investigating is certainly worth your time. Call your Landmarks Commission, city planner and/or archives office; they will clarify many questions and also provide excellent, current information.

1. *The National Register of Historic Places*
Your first move will be to find out if your property is listed in *The National Register*. If it is, you qualify immediately.

First, consult the cumulative listing of *National Register* properties in *The Federal Register*, which is shelved in most large libraries. If you cannot find the listing, go to step number two. If you do find it, jump to step number six.

2. Write to: U.S. Department of the Interior
Heritage Conservation and Recreation Service
The National Register of Historic Places
Washington, D.C. 20243

Ask if your property is listed in *The National Register,* either individually or as a part of a historic district. The only information necessary to give is the address of your property.

Ask also for a brochure (free) about *The National Register* and a list of State Historic Preservation Offices (SHPO's).

If you are advised that you are indeed in *The National Register,* you can proceed to step number six. Otherwise, continue with step number three.

3. Write to your State Historic Preservation Office (SHPO) and make the following inquiry:

Is your property located in a historic district under a state statute? If not, can the SHPO give you the address of the local historic-sites commission pertaining to your area?

4. After having received the information that your property is not listed by the SHPO, write to the appropriate local historic-sites commission and ask if your property is located in a historic district under a local statute.

5. If you discover that your property is not listed by any of the above sources, you do not qualify for tax incentives.

There is one remaining possibility: if you believe that your property—or the district in which it is located—should be placed on *The National Register,* you should write again to your SHPO, requesting a review of the property or the district for possible nomination to *The National Register.* This request normally results in a referral to the SHPO representative authorized to make formal request for certification.

6. If your property is listed, you will need the following materials to obtain certification for tax incentives:

A. Historic Preservation Certification Application.

There are two parts to this application. Part I pertains to the structure itself, and the application does not have to be completed by owners if the property is listed individually in *The National Register.*

All owners complete Part II pertaining to the rehabilitation work itself.

B. The Secretary of the Interior's "Standards for Rehabilitation."

C. Information sheets entitled,"Tax Reform Act Incentives and Disincentives" and "The Tax Reform Act of 1976."

D. Brochure entitled "Tax Incentives for Rehabilitating Historic Buildings."

E. Additional information pertaining to the "Tax Reform

Act of 1976" and the "Revenue Act of 1978," i.e., an investment tax credit for rehabilitation of commercial or industrial structures.

Information listed in A and B may be obtained by writing:
Office of Archaeology and Historic Preservation
Heritage Conservation and Recreation Service
U.S. Department of the Interior
Washington, D.C. 20240

The materials you will be receiving are easy to understand, are provided free of charge, and will arrive likely within two weeks of your request.

Once you have studied them, you will probably be prepared to proceed with the application (only five pages) on your own. However, for filing your income tax return, you are advised to consult your tax counsel to assist in determining the specific tax consequences.

Taxes of all kinds are critical elements in your planning and in the future success of your business. You and a qualified tax adviser together should be able to obtain the best results for your investment venture or business enterprise. It pays to look at taxes; the proper application of tax laws can be to your advantage. (A dollar saved is extra income for you).

Ready To Renovate

8 "First Things First"

The contract has been signed. You have the keys (if there are any) in your pocket and visions of gleaming brass doorknobs dancing in your head. In your mind's eye, you know just the pattern of wallpaper that you will hang in the foyer, and the exact style of vanity to enhance the bathroom. You have ideas for colors and for curtains and what kind of carpets you will lay. In short, you are a walking, creative agglomeration.

Now stop. Before you walk in the door, gather up all of these ideas and tuck them away where they will be safe until later. Hang on to your energy and your imagination; you will need them for

44

the laborious, first phase of the renovation that will often be drudgery.

The Clean-up

Do not let this awesome task overwhelm you. The process of renovation is a one-step-at-a-time project, and the first step is to strip your "investment" of everything but its charming, virgin shell.

You may be extremely fortunate to follow in the wake of tenants or former owners who were neat, and left the house tidy and clean, but this is the exception. Most structures to be renovated are full of trash, dust, stained and filthy carpets, peeling wallpaper, and decaying linoleum. While one is always anxious to get on with the more glamorous aspects of renewal, usually it is necessary to spend the first days in old clothes.

Why should one clean up before the workmen arrive? "They will only mess up again!" Good question. Unfortunately, few contractors will even bid on a debris-filled house. The one who does will ordinarily give you a cost-estimate that is excessively high. He will include the price of cleaning up in the total costs of repair or will add twenty per cent to cover unseen problems that may be masked by the debris.

The best approach is to plunge directly into this unpleasant but necessary chore. Normally, allow a week for cleaning a large house and yard, spending two and one-half days on each. If the place is small, spend three days total. You can choose to do the work yourself or hire others to help you.

If you decide on enlisting additional hands, think about students or other non-professionals. They are a good source, provided you define tasks clearly and supervise or join in as the work is being done.

The best advice is not to use professional house-cleaning companies. They are expensive and are rarely equipped for the overwhelming job of house cleaning at this point. Occasionally, you might employ crews from manpower/day-labor pools, but you may have mixed success with them. If you choose to utilize this kind of labor, it is recommended that you stress to the dispatcher that you want reliable, hard-working, stronger persons, if possible. Be prepared to supervise continually. Emphasize that you will terminate loafers. Beware of hiring a large crew and dispersing them throughout the house, as you cannot be everywhere at once to supervise. Instead, hire a small crew and keep them working on one area at a time. Prepare, in advance, a list of jobs to be done so that you are always ready with an answer to the question, "What do we do next?" Be assured that your own participation in the work effort will serve as a motivation to the crew, as well as being a time and money saver for you.

What follows is a suggested procedure for the clean-up:

1. Have on hand plenty of cleaning supplies and equipment. Necessary for doing the job are buckets, brushes, rags, putty knives, large, heavy-duty trash bags, brooms, dust pans, scouring pads, window cleaner, mops or sponge mops, hose vacuum, small vacuum brushes, electrical plug adapters, rakes, hoes, small brushes (even a toothbrush), razors and blades, paper towels, small trash cans and large cardboard cartons (from stores), and chemical cleaners.

2. List jobs to be done in each room and those outside.

3. Pick up your cleaning crew, if you are hiring one.

4. Open all windows in the house to let out the stale air and let in the fresh.

5. Remove debris.

6. If the debris is more than can be discarded in trash bags or large cartons, rent a dumpster or other trash container (available through local trash-collection agencies).

7. Remove all carpets or old rugs that are to be replaced.

8. Remove worn-out linoleum-tile floor coverings. (If they should be in good condition, you may wish to keep them).

9. Remove carpet-tack stripping and nails in floors.

10. Take down draperies, curtains, blinds and window hanging hardware.

11. Tear off any loose-hanging or sagging wallpaper.

12. Clean the bathrooms; wash tile, fixtures, floors and walls.

13. Scrape flaking paint from walls, woodwork, doors, windows, floors.

14. Wash down all badly soiled walls and woodwork to remove heavy dirt, grease and oil. Do not wash areas that are only moderately soiled; painting will take care of that problem.

15. Wash windows inside and out.

16. Sweep house thoroughly.

17. Wash floors by the best but hardest way— down on your hands and knees—with plenty of rags, brushes and soapy water. (A

less humbling method is the use of brushes with a long handle). Rinse floors well and then wipe completely dry. Take care against soaking hardwood or heart-pine flooring; excess water and non-drying may cause the boards to buckle.

18. Remove trash from the yard.

19. Trim heavy tree and bush branches that are close to the house in positions that will impede workmen. At this point, do not spend money on landscaping; that will come later.

20. Bid farewell to the debris and have it hauled away.

21. Finally, remember that a thorough clean-up will have to take place after the renovation.

Security

You might think the act of locking up an empty, dilapidated house would have a low priority in the early stages of renovation. After all, what is there to steal? Though there are probably few treasures to lose at this time, there are windows that can be broken, fixtures that, if retained, might emerge priceless when cleaned and polished, and interiors that could be damaged badly by vandals. This is especially true in renovated houses, left vacant for years. Also, in a very short time, there will be items of value in the house and costly decorating to be protected. Perhaps more significant is the questionable insurability of a structure that is not secured properly.

Begin the security task by checking to see if there are any

good, working locks on all exterior entranceways. If not, the problem must be attended to; if there are locks, have several keys made and then be sure to keep a list of the individuals to whom they have been assigned. This includes contractors; make sure they return the keys when their job is completed.

Repair or replace broken windows. A lock on the door would be meaningless if there is a smashed window pane or a large hole in the side of the house.

Enlist the help of the local police. Many municipalities keep records of vacant houses (often called the "Vacation House List"), enabling police squad cars to make extra patrols at these sites. Too, a town sometimes has a "Home Security System," a special agency, usually located in the courthouse, whose sole function is to secure and protect houses. In many cases, this agency will provide all the labor that is involved in replacing or adding locks to windows and doors. All the owner pays for is the cost of the materials. This can mean a huge savings in both time and dollars.

Neighbors can be of great help as well. Most are eager to lend a hand to the "shining knights" who are going to raise property values by transforming the neighborhood "problem" into a fine residence.

If you do not have a business card, type your name, address, and telephone number on a 3x5 card. If you have an office number, include that, too. Also, add the telephones of the police and fire departments. Introduce yourself to the neighbors, explain briefly your plans for renovation of the structure, and ask them to please call you if they note any unusual activity around the house. Let them know that you will have contractors and workmen on the site but would appreciate being alerted to any suspicious activity.

Termites And Pests—Less Evictable Tenants

There may be a few residents in the house you have purchased to renovate that are undaunted by locks and bolts. Your next step, then, is to call a reputable exterminator to determine the extent of your problem. Termites, of course, are the most devastating. While the damage done by these hungry critters is usually correctable, in severe cases restoration can be expensive. If possible, it is wise to procure an inspection before you purchase the house, so that you can adjust the cost to allow for the necessary repairs. Most firms specializing in termite control will also oversee the repair or replacement of the foundation and beams. When the time comes for you to sell, you may be required to submit a "Termite Letter" or a "Termite Bond," which states that the house is free from termites and structural damage.

If other pests—roaches or rats, for instance—are also on the premises, have them exterminated. They may not cause any structural damage, but can be very disconcerting to workmen, not to mention prospective buyers.

Preliminary Renovation Decisions

Now, is it time to start calling contractors? Not quite.

A great deal of your time and the contractor's can be saved if you have decided what you want done before he or any other workmen arrive to make their bids. Do not have a contractor stand around while you are pondering whether the living room should be painted blue or white, or if the kitchen would look better painted or with flowered wallpaper. Know, also, if special brand-name paints[5] will be used, so that the contractor can place his order immediately.

Acquire a notebook or a three-ring binder with plenty of dividers. Designate a section for each room of the project or each topic (like plumbing, electrical, light fixtures, paint inside and out), then keep an orderly, detailed list of decisions and specifications.

Begin by walking through and around the house, systematically noting every project that has to be completed in the interior and on the exterior of the home. Your list should include items to be reconstructed or repaired, windows needing replacement, floors to be refinished, fixtures to be replaced or repaired, exact colors of paint, details of woodwork painting or refinishing, rooms to have wallpaper, and the precise extent of major remodeling in kitchens and bathrooms.

Handymen *versus* Professionals

Naturally there is an economic advantage in doing some of the renovation work yourself. If you are renovating a place you plan to live in for many years, you have the luxury of time to learn the necessary skills to complete a number of tasks. On the other hand, if your plans are a short-term renovation and a speedy, profitable sale, that is a different matter. Each dollar you save as a do-

[5]Paints such as Devoe Charleston, or Williamsburg colors, are used frequently in house restorations, especially in eastern United States.

it-yourselfer may well end in the hands of your banker because of the carrying costs of misspent weeks.

Also, experience reveals that non-professional work often winds up looking non-professional. Appraisers and prospective buyers have extremely sharp eyes. If your renovation is a side-venture to your regular employment, you may find yourself biting off more than you can chew—working an eight-hour day and a six-hour evening. With this kind of schedule, your nerves may become frayed, your patience may lag, and you may begin taking short cuts that will result in second-class workmanship.

Excepting in areas in which one feels that he/she is highly skilled and confident of good results, use professionals, meanwhile endeavoring to learn as much as you can while the renovation proceeds. Each renovation which you handle leaves you better equipped to communicate effectively with contractors and, by observing carefully, you can pick up skills that may enable you to perform some of the labor in the future.

Finding A Contractor

And **now** you are ready to start calling contractors.

During your first renovation effort, you will make more calls than you will ever need to make again. Quickly, you will develop your own list of contractors whose work is commendable, who are dependable, and whose prices are fair. For your first "walk through the yellow pages," here are some tips:

1. Check out a contractor's reputation if you have not dealt with him before; ask for references; follow up on them.

2. Beware of the contractor who comes to your door "because he is doing work in the neighborhood."

3. Steer clear of the contractor who has no known address or telephone number.

4. Do not deal with one who requests a large portion of the total price in advance.

5. When practical, obtain at least three **written** estimates for every job. Specific details regarding materials and workmanship should be outlined. Remember that a paint job is not just a paint job and unless you specify two coats of oil paint, you may get only one. If the job is not completed to specifications, you should not have to pay the full price.

6. Think about the fact that a contractor has to make a profit, too. Look for a price, not inflated, but one that does allow for a fair

profit for the contractor.

7. Insist that the estimate include a "starting" and "completion" date. Indicate to the contractor that you will be flexible if extenuating circumstances (weather and natural disasters) should occur, but that you will expect the schedule to be adhered to. Time is money!

8. **Remember that the highest price does not necessarily mean the highest quality.** If you pay for a Cadillac, be sure you get one.

9. Work out payment schedules in advance. Some contractors require no money until the job is completed. Employ this type, if possible. Others prefer a small down payment, with the remainder to be paid at intervals during the work. If this is the case, withhold the final payment until the job is completed to your full satisfaction.

10. Be prepared to be flexible. Older structures hold surprises and if the contractor encounters one, he may add costs to the original estimate. You certainly do not want him to paint over a decayed porch plank.

11. Always inspect the work carefully during daylight hours. Beware of the contractor who requests that you pay him because "the hour is late," promising to "return tomorrow if there are any problems." You may never see him again.

12. If your agreement specifies that the work crew will clean up after the renovation, make sure that this is done before you pay.

13. Some contractors prefer a "cost plus" contract to protect them against sudden increases in the price of materials or labor. Much better for you is a firm price. "Cost plus" contracts nearly always live up to their title, with emphasis on the "plus."

14. Do not be hesitant about asking for a warranty on materials and workmanship.

15. Do not depend on only one contractor. Have several that you trust in each of the skilled areas, i.e., electrical, roofing, carpentry, plumbing, painting, and others, so that you will have alternatives if a company should go out of business, move, or become too busy for you. This also holds true for suppliers and materials. Pricing policies change constantly; comparison shopping can add to your potential profit. Do not let "familiarity" prevent you from obtaining the best price on identical or similar merchandise, or labor. On the other side of the coin, it is not recommended to change contractors just to save a few dollars on one

51

job. Loyalty runs two ways.

16. If your estimate does not include each and every item required for a particular project, ask for a revised estimate.

17. Evaluating, once the estimates are in, is one of the most difficult parts of a renovation. Not all contractors are consistent in their pricing. Some painters do not like three-story houses; some plumbers hate having to replace bathtubs; and some electricians have phobias against chandeliers. Thus, they may overquote deliberately on those jobs. Try to spot eccentric contractors and avoid them and their inflated prices.

18. Wrap-up a contractor's future abiding loyalty by **paying on time.** You will want him for your next renovation.

19. Act confidently! **Never** make such comments as "I don't know anything about plumbing." Assume the air that you do, and be decisive. However, refrain from making expensive choices if you are totally in the dark. Find out the facts first. As time goes on, you will become more adept at the lingo of skilled professionals.

20. Demand quality. Your reputation as a renovator hangs in the balance.

Tips On Supervising Contractors And Work Crews

1. Stay on the site as much as possible, and cloak yourself with the knowledge and expertise in whatever job is being undertaken.

2. Be prepared to do a little prodding as the work nears its end. Contractors, like the rest of us, become a little bored with the last ten per cent of work to be done. They are ready to go on to something new and will, sometimes, even forego the last payment just for the privilege of moving on. Stay behind them if you spot the gypsy in their souls.

3. Try to schedule contractors so that they are on the site at different times. Contractors tend to bicker; they get in each other's way. The painter may come to you and say, "I would have had the bathroom painted on time if the plumber (who, by the way, is in Florida) had not made such a mess of the bathroom."

4. Despite your well-laid plans, you can still expect days of mass confusion. For example, the electrician has been scheduled for Tuesday, the plumber for Thursday, but both arrive on Wednesday. You will have to act as coordinator and referee.

As the actual renovation project begins, you should have a clear idea of your goals. Are you looking for short cuts to a quick, inexpensive renovation? If so, your future in the business may be short-lived. Or, will you demand comprehensive repairs, using top-quality materials and skills? If so, you will find that the job gets done as it should be done and in the best professional manner.

Whether you are renovating a house for yourself or are planning to sell for profit, a poorly installed bathroom appliance or a cheap paint job, to cite two deficiencies, will come back eventually to haunt you. Either you will be required to re-do the work a short time later, or your business reputation will suffer. Bear in mind, your first renovated house will help to sell your second and third (as the word passes among satisfied buyers).

This is not to say that you should ignore money-saving approaches and plausible cost-cutting methods. But never choose an inexpensive technique if it is also inferior. Pretend that you are the future occupant; settle for no less than you would demand.

9 From The Outside In

The drudgery of cleaning up and rejuvenating the interior may be exceeded only by the tedious requirements of the second part of renovation—exterior repairs.

You will have made sure that the structure is sound before attempting the interior. Otherwise, you might as well hang wallpaper on an eggshell.

The procedure for exterior restoration varies according to schedules of contractors and the nature of the work to be done. Depending on geographical locale, your renovation may also be subject to such weather conditions as a January cold spell that freezes, literally, all exterior efforts.

Listed here are the tasks to be done in the general order of cost, based on reliable experience, beginning with the most expensive.

The Roof

There are three main reasons for replacing a roof. A hole is quite obviously the first. Either the roof is leaking or will do so within a short time. Second is the likelihood that an aged roof will lower the appraisal figure when you are ready to sell the house.

The third reason is appearance. Nothing ages a house quite as noticeably as a roof that for years has been exposed to sun, rain, snow, ice, storms, wildlife, pineneedles and so on. A stained, dirty roof, no matter how inherently sound, will detract appreciably from the aesthetic and, therefore, from the real value of the property. Further, in all but a few cases, trying to clean a discolored roof is a lackluster and futile approach; the results are not satisfactory and the roof's appearance remains marginal.

Results are dramatic with a new roof[6] and, in most cases, you will be able to recoup your investment. ("The house has a new roof" are sweet words to a prospective buyer).

You must acquire some basic knowledge and a little lingo before contacting roofing contractors: first, shingles are priced by the square and a square is a section measuring ten-by-ten feet. (The cost of materials will be based on the price per square for the shingles you select).

Labor is another matter, and a contractor's bid will vary according to the pitch and style of the roof, with a steeper pitch obviously costing more to shingle.

To evaluate roofing estimates once you have them in hand, make a call to a roofing supply company to ask the price per square of the shingles you have selected. Afterward, ask your contractor, "How many squares is this estimate based on?" You can then compare his bid with the actual cost of materials and figure his charges for both materials and labor. This will also afford you a comparison between roofing contractors.

Be informed on local building codes for roofs. Many towns have a "two-ply" code, which means simply that there can be only two layers of roofing materials on a roof at one time. If you are forced to replace a two-layered roof, you will have to strip the old material before adding the new. By ignoring the code, you risk a future visit from an irate building inspector who will force you to jerk off your brand-new roof from your lovely, newly renovated mansion.

Again, as with other projects, you must be prepared for surprises and flexible to their costs. A roofer may discover ruined planks under old shingles; these must be replaced before he can continue. Therefore, be ready for on-the-spot negotiations.

---

[6] Asphalt shingles are preferable. Choose such neutral shades as grey or black for their compatibility with a wide variety of paint colors.

Foundation

Second is the foundation which is listed in that order because experience has shown that it is not the most costly (if you have avoided purchasing a house that appeared to have severe foundation problems). If you do have a project with severe foundation problems, it becomes a priority and is sure to gobble up a sizeable share of renovation funds. If you fail to repair a faulty foundation, you will either be chasing and replastering wall cracks forever or be struggling to save your reputation as a renovator from the wrath of your unfortunate buyer.

Begin by checking under the house for foundation walls and piers which may have shifted. Check to see if piers may have tilted or been smashed down by previous repairs. (Good tools for such repairs are metal jacks that can be used to level sagging floors, expensive but vital).

If the only structural damage is that which has occurred from termites, the termite-control firm you will hire will be equipped to correct the problem, using its own sub-contractors. If the work should fall within the province of brick masons and foundation carpenters, costs will skyrocket.

At the risk of your appearing hindsighted, it is stressed that you avoid a house altogether that must be rebuilt from the bottom up.

Waterproofing is a matter of priorities. Certainly you will never sell a house for which the buyer needs hip boots to tour the basement. On the other hand, minor seepage and moisture in an old home is often a matter of course and may or may not be of concern to your prospective occupants. A waterproofing company can give you advice on the extent of the correction required. While the most common type of correction is exterior waterproofing, minor leakage can also be alleviated with special waterproofing paint applied to interior walls. This could be a worthwhile investment since it will spruce up a dingy-looking basement at the same time.

Gutters

There was a past era of home construction when gutters were as American as apple pie. Every house had them and no one ever questioned their utility. Now, it has become evident that many structures do not need gutters at all, and that is why careful examination should be undertaken before one elects automatically to repair or replace worn-out gutters and downspouts. If the house you are renovating has gutters[7] in good condition or need only slight repairs and minor replacements, you will probably want to keep them. If they are in poor condition, you can replace all, some, or have none.

Investigate the house carefully. Are the gutters performing a viable function by draining water away from the house and its foundation? Or, does the house have such a wide overhang that, were the gutters removed, the rain would still fall away? If so, the gutters are probably nonessential. Perhaps you will find that some gutters are serving a proper function, others are contributing nothing but a catch-all for trash. Remove the drones and replace with workers.

At one time, concealed gutters were built into the edge of the roof-line and were the rage. This type is a real leaf and debris collector and will cause severe roof damage eventually.

If gutters are called for, they should be installed as unobtrusively as possible. Do not place downspouts in the center; choose a corner where walls meet instead. Paint gutters and downspouts to match the walls or the trim they transect.

Porches Or Piazzas

House designs have gone through varying periods when porches or piazzas[8] have been in and out of vogue. Their almost total disappearance has been, however, a rather recent phenomenon during which builders decided that most people would prefer a deck or a patio, covered or uncovered, normally placed at the rear by the house. While there is nothing wrong with patios or decks, they do not preclude the functional appeal of a porch.

Many times, too, renovators have decided to tear away porches in excellent condition because they were convinced that the porch "dated" the house. In so doing, they lost valuable living space instead of having renovated the porch to a form that would have

---

[7] During one renovation project, the authors asked a contractor for his opinion on how frequently gutters would require cleaning. Comparing the location with that of his home, he estimated twice per month. Envisioning twenty-four trips a year to scoop junk out of the gutters, they thanked him politely for his advice, then concluded that the gutters would add nothing but chores to the new owner's investment.

[8] In some historic cities such as Charleston, South Carolina, they are designated as piazzas, occasionally, verandahs.

enhanced the house both architecturally and functionally, and added to its value.

If a porch located at the rear or the side is adaptable to being screened or glassed in, it can be built with removable panels for extreme seasons: a screened porch for summer; glassed in for winter; and/or turned into a solarium and plant room. Heating and air conditioning should be extended into the area with vents that can be shut off when heating or cooling is not needed. The area becomes most attractive when floors are covered with a good grade of indoor-outdoor carpeting or ceramic tile, the walls and ceilings are painted or wallpapered, and good lighting installed. An excellent feature to consider is the combination light-ceiling fan (rather costly but worth it) which can be acquired in many decorative styles, with interesting effects, and types of circulation.

Should the house have been constructed on a narrow lot with other homes close on either side, owners seldom use their front porch because of lack of privacy. However, this can be remedied by installing two lattice panels on each side-end of the porch to provide very effective screening. The porch then can become a favorite living area.

For any porch retained as is, some repairs may be required. Decayed planks or rotted banisters should be replaced, using lumber designed for this purpose. If trees shade the porch, preventing rapid drying of steps after a rainfall, each of the steps should be reconstructed using two planks with a narrow space in between for drainage. They should be painted on both sides before installation to protect the wood on the underside, too.

Wooden porches can be a headache to maintain; and durable, deck paint should be used on them. Polyurethane paints are also excellent for this purpose. If you are replacing an entire porch floor with new wood, you might choose a good, protective stain which will not chip or flake as paint does. Neutral colors, grey, black or white, will fight fewer battles with the house's exterior color scheme, but many times the color is the same as "accent" wood (like shutters) on the house.

Preparation For Painting

Survey the house to locate all areas where clapboard has fallen off or has decayed or warped. Have damaged boards replaced or, if good enough, nailed back into place. Facing boards and overhangs are particularly susceptible to damage because water often collects there. Replace rotted ones. Check all brick work for mortar which may have dried out and fallen away. Then repair with new mortar and new brick, if necessary. Check corners of the structure to insure there has been no pulling away. Most decay and damage can be seen but do not trust sight alone. Some parts appear sound, yet have the consistency of balsa wood. Have a contractor go over the house, hammer-tapping all wooden surfaces for decay. Few discoveries are more disheartening than that one the painter calls down suddenly from his ladder, "Hey, there's a big decayed area up here under the overhang; what do you want me to do, paint over it?"

You will, of course, tell him to paint around that area; meanwhile, you must get in touch with the previous contractor, asking him to return to repair the part that you—or he—should have spotted initially. Such mistakes are costly and also time-consuming, not to mention annoying.

Exterior Painting

Painting the exterior of the house before you tackle the inside may seem a bit like putting your coat on before your sweater when you are dressing to go out. But the sooner you can make the exterior presentable, the better. It lifts your spirits and the neighbors will love it. Even contractors and other workmen seem happier with a new paint job. Additionally, prospects may stop by much sooner, giving you resale possibilities at an earlier date.

Inside, you can be proceeding with other major projects like heating and air conditioning, plumbing and electrical work.

This sequence is conditional; weather is a big factor that could delay exterior house-painting for several weeks or months. You will also be apprized, as you gather bids for interior work, that some inside tasks will mar the outside of the house slightly. For example, plumbing restoration may involve installation of pipes to or from the outside or the electrical wiring may call for a box to be placed on an outside wall. You might elect to have all of these jobs completed first to avoid having the painters return for touch-up work.

Some painters prefer to do all the "readying" work themselves. (Readying is scraping off loose and flaking paint, caulking cracks, filling holes). Make sure you ask the contractor if his estimate includes these chores before you give him the job. If his bid does not, you will have to find someone to do it. Although this is dirty, slow work, it is absolutely necessary since cracked, baked-on paint will show through the new coats.

Obtain estimates from at least three painters and follow the same evaluating process as you would for other projects. Insist that exterior painters prime all new wood and any other area where paint has flaked away completely leaving old wood bare. Also, require that new wood, especially in large areas, receive an additional spotting-coat of primer, with shellac sealer added on knots in the wood (to prevent sap from the knots eventually bleeding through).

Selecting paint for the exterior is time-consuming and nerve-racking.[9] It pays to be picky. It is best to begin by making a sketch of the house and testing paint chips on it. From these, make a preliminary decision of several possible colors, then have a gallon or smaller quantity, if your paint store will do this, of each color mixed. Using samples, test the paint on a part of the house where door, wall surface, and trim meet. After having painted the sample, examine the appearance over a period of several days and at different times during the day. Then, darken or lighten the shades and hues until you feel you have the right combination.

While there is a debate on this topic, oil-base paint is often preferred to latex because of its durability. It takes longer to apply but will tend to last longer. However, latex paint will cover old surfaces and minor flaws (small defects in outside wood, etc.) better than oil. On occasions, it is advisable to use a good quality latex

[9]The authors' final decision usually involves three colors, one for the body of the house, another for the trim, and a third for doors and shutters.

61

on exterior wood siding where, cost-wise, it would be imprac-
ticable to remove the old paint. Always, however, use oil base
paint on exterior trim (windows, doors, etc.). Flat paint, rather than
a semi-gloss, will minimize flaws better, especially on siding.

It is never wise to try to purchase a custom paint color from a
large chain or department store[10] since their colors change and
may be difficult to duplicate.

Always select paint well in advance of the day the painters are
expected to arrive. Also, over-order slightly. The paint that is left
over is labeled "exterior," "doors and shutters," and so on, and is
presented to the new owners for matching touch-ups later on.

[10]Sometime ago during one of the authors' first renovations, while using a chain store
product, they discovered that the clerk had badly underestimated the amount of paint that
would be necessary for the exterior of a brick house. When they ran out of paint, only the
back and one side of the structure had been completed. They returned for more and the
second batch proved to be several shades off from the original. The store mixed a third,
with the same results. Finally, an employee from a local paint and decorating firm, using
the sample the authors had brought, was willing to hand-mix enough paint to finish the job.
Needless to say, that firm is now patronized exclusively.

10 The Interior Of The House

Your castle is now tight from its top to the bottom, and it gleams with a fresh, new color. It is time to see what is happening indoors.

The inner workings of your house are running like a top—the furnace is purring and churning out nice warm air into rooms snugly insulated, or air conditioning is flowing through ducts; water is swilling through pipes; and voltage is traveling along safe, updated wires.

Now, for the same reasons as before when you did not hang wallpaper under a leaky roof, you have to tighten up the structure's "inners," and inspect and correct, if necessary, any safety hazards before proceeding with the renovation-cosmetics.

Heating And Air Conditioning

A reasonably modern heating/air conditioning system is essential if you want to obtain maximum profit from the renovated house. "Reasonably" means that a twenty-year-old cast-iron, gas furnace is all right provided it is functioning properly and economically. If not, then you must decide to what extent you will go in making repairs or adding a replacement.

It is wise to obtain several opinions on the system already there. Be wary of contractors who are quick to levy a death sentence on one because it is old. True, it could last only a few days; on the other hand, it might last for years. When seeking the advice of heating and air conditioning contractors, ask specific questions. Try to discern how much of the existing system is acceptable; how much must be replaced. Avoid a contractor who tells you instantly the system is going to explode any minute. He may be trying to frighten you into buying a new or larger system than is required. Heating systems can often be repaired. Make it clear that you would like to explore this alternative before you give the signal to scrap it, before you spend indiscriminately.

There will be, of course, other considerations. Is the present system too costly to operate? Would the installation of a more economical unit, if the old one is an oil furnace, be wise? Should you convert to natural gas or install an electric heat pump to bring a savings potential that might attract a prospective buyer?

Where the age of a system becomes more significant is the question of air conditioning. If the house is located in a climate where air conditioning is almost as important as food and water, you will need to consider its addition. Questions—is the present heating system adaptable to the installation or addition of air conditioning; are ducts adequate, if not, how extensive would be the required ductwork; is the house's electrical service capable of supporting the cooling system required? If the structure is located in a northern clime where air conditioning may be a luxury used less frequently, you will want to weigh the cost of a cooling system with the value it will bring at resale.

Comfortable temperatures are of inestimable benefit to your contractors renovating your property during extreme winter or summer temperatures. As you can see, adequate working conditions are conducive to a higher quality and quicker completion, both being to your financial advantage.

64

Plumbing

There is an old saying about vintage kitchens and bathrooms, "They are nice places to visit, but you wouldn't want to live there." While buyers would adore having a bedroom about which they could say "George Washington slept here," they want a bathroom and a kitchen resplendent of the twentieth century. If you have one in the house you buy to renovate, you might wish to retain the popular, priceless, claw-footed bathtub or beautiful pedestal sink. If so, make sure the fixtures are gleaming (or able to be so) and that **all** fixtures are totally functional.

Have a reputable contractor check all of the plumbing in the house, including under-the-house pipes, as well as fixtures in bathrooms and in the kitchen. Usually, you will find that the incoming pipes and the drainage pipes are in good condition. Occasionally, interior water pipes will need replacing.

Faulty plumbing is not ordinarily caused by faulty pipes. More often than not, the moving parts are to blame. Variety stores' items, such as flusher bulbs and aerators, may be the only culprits in what at first appears to be a monumental problem.

Before the plumber arrives, make a detailed list of broken fixtures and any items you might want to replace for aesthetic appearance. Broken commodes, sinks, tubs, showers and faucets must be replaced automatically. Do not spend time or money trying to clean badly stained sinks and tubs or those with lots of chipped porcelain; they always end up looking like old, worn-out, half-cleaned sinks and tubs. Replace them! Even if you should not replace the commode itself, always install a new seat. Exceptions to this replacement rule might be existing tubs and sinks that can be refurbished, or claw-footed tubs that can be restored with new porcelain or paint.

For new fixtures, know your color schemes before you call the plumber. By visiting a plumbing supply outlet or perusing a few catalogs, you might be able to decide on advance orders.[11] Remember that the plumber charges to walk in the door. Make it your goal to have him complete his business in a minimum of

---

[11]From their experience with bathroom and kitchen renovation, the authors have learned that there are some modern touches that can be skirted with little or no value-loss. For example, they do not always add showers in bathrooms that do not have them. They have, however, explored the addition cost-wise and if a prospective buyer complains about the absence of a shower, they are prepared to demonstrate how moderate the installation would be if desired. The same can be true of disposals and trash compactors, not found in every modern home today.

visits, one, if possible. If there are no serious problems, and if you are prepared, he can complete his work on a one-shot basis.

Never replace fixtures because of color alone; only if they are broken. If fixtures are a ghastly color, select a wallpaper or a paint tone that will subdue or complement them. Among the thousands of kinds of wallpapers available, there is usually one that can make almost any fixture look acceptable. If you need to start over with fixtures in a bath, white is the best color—allowing the prospective buyer more choices in decoration.

Electrical Work

Older houses are vulnerable especially to electrical problems; few built over fifty years ago have circuits sufficient to carry the power load for today's appliance craze. In addition to heating and/or air conditioning, electrical systems have to accommodate electric ranges, microwaves, televisions and stereos, washers and dryers, numerous housecleaning and cosmetic devices, and extra lighting. All these require re-evaluation of the amp service into the house and of the fuse box or circuit-breaker panel.

Safety is paramount. While older houses do require the most expenditures in this regard, newer ones are not arbitrarily safe from electrical problems. For example, some houses that were built between 1965 and 1974 were constructed using aluminum wiring. There are some serious questions about the safety of this wire.[12]

Electrical work is costly, more so when pulling wires through walls of older homes. An alternative is to have outside wiring enclosed in an aluminum conduit, cutting down labor and expense. However, the job must be done expertly, with the conduit concealed if at all possible and painted the same color as the house's exterior.

Be sure to instruct your electrical contractor to submit a full estimate for a safely wired, adequate service. As with the plumbing contractor or any other, try to have all estimating done in one service call, though you may need the electrician to return later to install lighting fixtures.

Know in advance where you will place fixtures and wall outlets. In kitchens, try to add plugs in convenient places for blend-

---

[12]The Consumer Product Safety Commission, Washington, D.C. 20207 offers a free booklet describing how you can tell whether or not a house has aluminum wiring and whether or not it is safe.

ers, toasters, mixers, and other small appliances, and outlets in bathrooms for electric razors, hair dryers, and so on.

Better building codes recommend—and some require—at least one outlet per wall in every room and two on long walls. If not absolutely mandated by the building code, these are contingent upon the room design and possible furniture placement. Some may be omitted if too costly.

You will discover that many older houses have valuable brass lighting fixtures hiding behind a veil of black tarnish or paint. How can you tell if it is real brass? If a magnet will not stick to it, the fixture is probably brass. In many cases, it is less costly to clean than to replace. Do not forget to check the wires for safety.

Choose silent switches; install dimmer switches where adjustment of lighting is desirable. To save energy, add flourescent lights in the kitchen and in other possible places; however, have sufficiently bright lights in the bathrooms. The decor of a dining room is greatly embellished with a chandelier but its style should be in keeping with the architecture of the house. An attractive light fixture is a good sales feature. In all rooms, use only the most tasteful fixtures, those that are in correct proportion to the size and character of the room.

When purchasing lighting fixtures, ask your supplier to agree to allow the new owner to exchange a fixture he does not particularly care for—an excellent point for you, the seller.

Insulation

The energy crisis has made insulation more of a necessity than an option. If the renovation budget permits, a total insulation job should be done, though it will not be inexpensive. The price will vary dependent upon the size, age and condition of the house and the climate in which it is located.

If total insulation is not possible, your first priority is the attic. Studies show that an attic without insulation allows as much as thirty-five per cent of winter heating to escape through the roof; older structures may need even more because of their greater heat loss. Even with attic insulation, a home may need more, especially if the existing insulation has settled by two to three inches. Next insulation priorities are storm windows, walls (blown-in-insulation), and floors. Costs will vary for kinds and amounts needed; thickness of walls; size and types of windows also enter into the price.

Knowledge about insulation can be confusing. First, one must understand the "R Value," which is the thermal resistance of a given material. It is a measure of the material's ability to retard the flow of heat from one surface to another. The higher the R Value, the more resistance.

Materials vary widely in their insulating qualities. Some studies have shown that one inch of mineral wool or fiberglass has the same insulating value as a brick wall thirty-four-inches thick or a concrete wall forty-seven-inches thick. The best guideline is to check with your local utility for the recommended R Value in your area.

In working with insulating contractors, you should obtain at least three written bids on the same R Value of the product you wish to use for areas of house to be insulated and the contractor's beginning and completion dates. It is best to request a breakdown of the price on each area to be insulated, as you may choose just one (i.e., attic) or two areas at this time. You can pass along the information you received on other areas to the purchaser. As in all bids, compare apples to apples and be fair to all parties concerned.

With insulation one of the main topics of the day, you may run into unethical tradesmen. You will be safe, though, if your contract states exactly what areas are to be insulated and what types of materials will be used, plus the R Value. Deal only with reputable, responsible vendors; beware of salespeople who make exorbitant claims of utility savings while playing down the cost you will incur.

Remember, too, that insulation has tax deductible aspects. Tax benefits may allow you to be a bit more comprehensive in your insulating efforts but avoid overdoing. Figure how much is necessary; calculate the amount that would take you beyond the point of diminishing returns.

Be mindful in all you do that work to improve wiring, plumbing, insulation, or other renovations does not come at a low price. Always try to make the best choice.

11 Putting On The "Make-up"

Once the groundwork of renovation has been laid, the cosmetic phase is fun and very rewarding. Results can be dramatic and fast. Wallpaper and paint turn pumpkins into dazzling carriages overnight. Finally, after having poured dollars into such less visible improvements as utility systems, insulation and other more technical projects, you can now direct your efforts toward the more beautiful endeavors. In decorating, you can become a real do-it-yourselfer, using your ingenuity, imagination and talents to achieve a bang-up job with a limited budget.

Be forewarned, though, that at times you can be dismayed. In the melee of paint, brushes, equipment of all sorts, rooms often look their very worst shortly before they are finished.

However, before cosmetic improvements can be undertaken, some clean-up must be done. If you are employing professionals for cleaning, you may have days when workers are stumbling over each other, followed by times in which no one arrives and progress is halted.

Some jobs take much longer than was anticipated; such delays are frustrating. Try scheduling contractors so that jobs will proceed in an orderly fashion but, even so, be prepared for breakdowns in your carefully planned agenda. You might as well know that your contractors may also be working on some of the other half-renovated houses around. Bear in mind, too, that some uncompleted renovations met their fates not for lack of funds but for loss of renovator patience, optimism, enthusiasm, and the willingness to carry on. This is true whether the renovator is an investor or an individual homeowner.

Avoid decorating too extensively. While the possibilities in any home are endless, you must make certain choices on the changes. Select those projects that will have a maximum upgrade effect and bring the largest profit at resale. Buyers are very discerning. A conservative approach, keeping within your budget while still making use of high-quality decorating techniques, will beat an inexpensive cover-up every time.

Floors

The repair, replacement and refinishing of floors is without question one of the single most important parts of house renovation. However, this should be done last to prevent the floors from being scratched while other renovation is in progress.

Look at floors as a series of space units rather than as total square-footage; different sections of a house require different solutions. Surprisingly, floors in older houses tend to be in better condition than those in more recently built ones. Heart-pine or hardwood floors, which most have, are usually undamaged either because they were well cared for or were covered with carpeting or area rugs.

Generally, it is not advisable to try and clean faded carpeting even though it may appear to be in acceptable condition. It will still look much the same. Instead, discard the floor coverings that you find throughout the house.

The worst areas in most houses are the kitchen, bathrooms, and laundry room where water has seeped through and ruined entire areas of flooring. Two, three or more successive layers of linoleum on a kitchen or bathroom floor is not unusual. Remove all, carefully inspect the floors underneath, and if there should be any damage, have it repaired. Where floors have been overlaid with carpeting[13] and are in good shape, have old tack stripping, tacks and nails removed, and then refinish the floors.

A sparkling, newly refinished **hardwood** floor in a renovated house makes a dramatic impression; however, the prospective purchaser can visualize how the rooms would look carpeted, should that be the preference.

---

[13]The authors do not dislike wall-to-wall carpeting but feel this is an option best left to the new owner's wishes as to color, grade, etc. More and more there is a return to the use of Oriental and other kinds of area rugs in older homes. They are especially beautiful against a stained floor, preferably a medium-dark walnut.

Find a good contractor who specializes in floor refinishing; ask him for a complete estimate in writing for cleaning, tack-strip and nail removal, sanding, if necessary, and applying at least two coats; one of stain, and one or two of varnish or polyutherane on the floors. However, some people prefer to wax instead. Specify clearly which floors he will be responsible for refinishing and at what price.

If you should be so fortunate that your house contains such asset-floors as parquet in the front areas, birch in the kitchen, slate in the entranceway, or marble in the bathrooms, investigate repair and restoration possibilities before you tear out any of these priceless items. Repairing, cleaning and refinishing an old birch floor or finding an expert craftsman who can repair slate or marble floors may not be the least expensive way to go but it is the best. For the written estimates on each of these jobs, list everything you need or think you might want done.

Kitchens

The kitchen is a primary gathering place in any house and should have an attractive, efficient arrangement for a twentieth-century lifestyle. It is also one of the most expensive parts to renovate; however, do not get so caught up in your renovation plans that you forget you are running a business or that you are an individual with just so much money to spend. You must balance what the purchaser may need against what the cost will be to you.

Old wallpaper must be stripped off. Walls and ceilings need to be scraped, cracks and other bad places replastered or repaired, and a white undercoat applied. If in the rare instance the walls should be board, all grease must be washed off and a primer applied. If kitchen cabinets can be salvaged, do so, but the majority of times, in older houses especially, they are dated, dirty and covered with multi-coats of paint. It pays (and costs less, too) to replace them with a medium-priced line of new cabinets. A plain white formica counter top and a stainless steel sink are attractive and go with nearly any kitchen decor.

Some purchasers of renovated houses may be put off by what appears to be an unfinished kitchen, but how far you should go in selecting paint, wallpaper, floor coverings, a range, a dishwasher, and lighting fixtures can be a big hassle. You will find prospective buyers who have very definite opinions on what they **will** have in their kitchens; if you have gone too far, they may reject your choices which conflict with their ideas. Nevertheless, a finished product is generally easier to sell.

Bathrooms

The same basic reasoning applies in renovating bathrooms.[14] Dated fixtures should be discarded for new ones, preferably white. Any damage to floors must be repaired and missing floor or wall tiles set, wallpaper stripped, wall areas scraped and undercoated.

Fireplaces

Home-heating costs have seen the resurgence of fireplaces, an increasingly valuable asset also appreciated aesthetically. In some older houses, there may be a fireplace in almost every room, requiring the decision on which to restore to working order and which should be closed and retained purely as decorative appointments. Repairs to existing chimneys and fireplaces are costly because they require not only materials but an artisan (they are in limited supply today). Also, fireplaces and chimneys are fire hazards and should be checked thoroughly by an expert. If building codes have been lax, all too frequently contractors would erect a wooden beam so close to the brickwork that a constant hot flame (over a long weekend or holiday or power outage) could cause the beam to ignite. Another problem is seepage of water into a chimney resulting in the mortar being alternately wet and dry and eventually deteriorating to the point of a fall out between chimney brick and fire brick. Evidence of these should be looked after thoroughly and, if found, defects must be repaired. Too, most older houses were built without mechanisms to close off a fireplace when not in use to prevent loss of heat or wildlife from entering. In making extensive repairs, you should install dampers.

Non-functional fireplaces should be sealed off to prevent their being used, and also to retain heat and/or air conditioning. It is no problem for a workman to unseal if someone wishes to restore them to working order. Seal them inside the chimney so they will give the warm beauty of a working fireplace to the room. Andirons, with logs placed on them, inside the fireplace gives an aesthetic lift

[14] Tile manufacturers have brought out as "style" some very unattractive colors of bathroom tile, and a surprising number of homes have them, for instance, what the authors refer to as "girdle pink" and "hospital green" and "blah beige." Their preference is white tile and white fixtures to make a bright, clean, first impression, allowing purchasers to use preferred color schemes and change them periodically.

to the area.

Call in a chimney sweep to clean the chimneys. The new owner will be pleased with the inspection/cleaning certificate you present to him.

Hearths also must be cleaned, repaired or replaced, and mantels should be restored to the best possible condition without deviating from their basic design. Marble mantels will have to be cleaned with care. Check your local building supply firm and get advice as to the best materials to use.

Many beautiful wooden mantels, when their numerous coats of paint are removed, reveal exquisite natural wood grain and texture and workmanship. If mantels are designed ornately, taking off the old, baked-on coats of paint will be extremely difficult. The "apply paint-remover, scrape" method is so tedious, you may be better advised to ask your contractor if the mantel could be removed easily and, if so, have it dipped by a commercial firm specializing in stripping furniture. One possibility is a furniture, dip-stripping firm with vats that are large enough to accommodate a sizeable mantel. Inquire into the cost before you have the mantel removed.

Simultaneously, you might consider removing ornate doors, interior and exterior shutters, and other intricate, architectural pieces and having them dipped, with re-installation included in the price.

Broken or missing frame-mouldings on mantels have to be replaced; and if the mantels are not dipped and refinished, they should be thoroughly cleaned.

Basements

The treatment in basement renovation involves sealing off all wall and floor leaks so that the area can be used for storage. If the lighting is defective, replace the wiring; if there is no light, install an inexpensive fixture. Replace unsafe stairways and tear down rickety, unsightly shelving. A thorough cleaning of the basement is a must, and adding a coat of paint on dirty stairs, stained or unsightly floors, walls and overhead areas, makes a substantial improvement. The basement is rarely occupied for living space, so renovation costs should be kept to a minimum. The purchaser will then be free to do with it what he pleases.

Attics

Attics receive about the same priority as basements. Check for safe stairs and adequate lighting, and clean the space thoroughly. Attics are handy for storage and also for additional living space (kids love it!) if the purchaser wishes.

Windows

Broken or stained windows and glasses, damaged sashes and unusable hardware must be replaced. As a rule, the decision is left to the buyer concerning the installation of bars or other security devices on ground-floor windows, doors and other places.

Interior Painting

In preparing the interior to be painted, walls and ceilings should be scraped or patched, plaster sanded (replaced, if necessary), and an undercoating of paint applied, if necessary. These will then be ready for the first coat of paint.

The choice of colors for the interior is a preferential choice depending upon a new owner's taste. The perfect solution is to leave the final coat until the last possible moment in the hope that a prospective purchaser will appear, decide to buy the house, and make the color choice. If this does not happen, select an off-white for use in residences; one or two unique colors for office space. If you select distinctive colors, the choices may turn out to be a good selling feature.

The same approach can be used with wallpaper, hoping for a purchaser who will decide the kind he/she wants. However, if you are selecting the wallpaper yourself, choose a color and design that will complement the basic design, age and style of the house and which will appeal to a broad spectrum of people. It pays to stay away from ultra-feminine or masculine patterns and use wallpaper with white backgrounds (easier, so trim can be painted white, too).

Laundry Room

If your "renovation house" is fortunate enough to have a laundry room, it could be turned into a real asset for the project. First, though, you must determine whether the area will be retained as a laundry room or utilized some other way. A determining factor will be whether you are renovating the structure as a residence, or for an office or other business use,[15] as each will have a different requirement.

Laundry rooms are normally small. If it is to be a laundry room, follow routine procedure of scraping walls, repairing windows and floors, covering the floor with a light, serviceable linoleum, painting the walls white (or using wallpaper to spruce up the room), and installing a functional, inexpensive, adequate light fixture. Make sure there are sufficient electrical outlets. Diagram the best arrangement for a washer and dryer, and install plumbing connection and vent.

Other handy uses for this room could be a pantry (if off kitchen); sewing room; husband or wife's office; child's play/craft room; children's study; or a small library.

Tell the prospective buyer about these possibilities. In renovating, it is important to make the most of what you have in a manner that opens alternatives for the buyer.

If the structure is being renovated in the expectation that it will be sold or leased as office space, take a slightly different approach. Imagine, for instance, what you would use the space for if the house were to be your offices, and then follow that lead. Several possibilities are a small office, a file room, copying machine space, kitchen break-area, storage or library. If it is determined that the most plausible use would be as a file or copying room, restore walls, floors, and so on, in the same procedure as if it were to be a laundry room. Plan for sufficient electrical plugs and have the electrician pull lines for both 110 and 220 power to accommodate most standard copying machines, if that will be the room's use. Adding this to the electrician's overall work is not very expensive and it creates an extra touch to lure the prospective buyer.

Add-ons And Additions

For individuals, if the space in your house is not adequate and there is a need for an extra bedroom and bath, you may decide it would be better to add-on rooms and renovate the whole residence rather than go through the process of buying a larger house, selling yours (perhaps paying income taxes on capital gain), having

---

[15]The authors have done both, with marked success.

higher house payments or paying a higher rate of interest.

"Add-on" has proven to be the best solution for many individuals and may well apply to the house where you make your home, whether it is the one you presently occupy or another you wish to renovate for your needs.

This approach does not work often for a company that is in the renovation/resale business.[16] The firm could find itself spending $12,000 or more to add a bedroom and bath to learn that the appraiser will allow only about $10,000 additional to the value of the house, leaving a dismal $2,000 loss. The best rule is to become involved only in a property renovation with good "as is" possibilities.

Vaulted Roofs And Ceilings

Moving advisedly, when renovating a medium-sized but not extraordinary house, it is possible to provide some special architectural interest through moderate remodeling. An excellent way is to tear out the low ceiling in a den, a living room, or in a dining room, to provide the room with a vaulted-roof ceiling effect. The cost is not prohibitive and the re-creation does make a very spectacular addition to an otherwise nondescript property. Remember to insulate properly.

Entranceways And Foyers

Entranceways and foyers are normally small but important parts in house restoration. Unless you are dealing with an old-style home with a tremendous hall, keep renovation plans simple but attractive.

The first impression upon entering a house is vital and can place the prospective purchaser in a positive frame of mind at once.

Follow standard procedures in renovating entranceways and foyers but try to give them some special attention. A pretty floor, more-expensive wallpaper (which is sensible if the area is small), and a distinctive lighting fixture are most important in making the

---

[16] The philosophy of the authors on this subject is very simple. They do not add-on rooms, work strictly with the space they have, and never purchase a house for renovation they feel would require an "add-on" or addition in order to make the house saleable. They do sometimes, however, convert a small, seldom used area into an additional bathroom if one is needed and they are convinced it will help immeasurably in the sale.

foyer or entranceway an asset. Another less expensive but very effective method for adding interest here is to use a distinctive color on the walls with woodwork painted a white or off-white.

Steps, Walks And Fences

Steps, walks and fences are three areas which should never be overlooked in renovation. Inasmuch as wooden steps have been found to be impractical, you may wish to replace them with good-looking brick ones, both for utility and beauty.

Broken or cracked walls surrounding the grounds should be repaired if possible; if not, totally replaced. Further, walls or fences—if they detract from the total outside appearance of the house—should be removed.

Adding Detail

An important consideration in every renovation project is what to remove and what to add. Considerably more interest and embellishment can be added to an otherwise square, boxlike dining room, entranceway or foyer by adding moulding around the ceiling or a chair rail on the walls. With these, an effective combination of paint and wallpaper creates a spacious, lovely effect.

Built-ins

In a great many houses, otherwise well-built, you will see poorly or amateurishly constructed built-ins like book shelves or inadequate storage spaces. If these are dirty but sound, clean and paint; if hardware is missing or mismatching, replace. The expense is worthwhile and will add much value to the house.

Landscaping

In pre-renovation cleaning, improve the yard immediately by cutting the grass, raking away leaves, trimming trees of dead branches, pruning back overgrown shrubs and bushes, and removing all trash.

Then comes the decision on what shrubs, if any, need to be added. Try to minimize such investment and follow the grounds budget (based on size of the yard) that you established very early in the game. Work with a reputable landscaper; ask him to achieve maximum effort for minimum cost. Think about setting out a few, small boxwoods or the like along a border area; other strategically placed evergreens at corners, ground covers and grass on bare lawn areas. It is possible to use pine bark or pebbles in difficult-to-plant places, and then accent the area with a shrub or two.

Hidden Treasures

You may discover intact, or at least repairable, hidden treasures[17] in a structure you are renovating—maybe even outdoors. Among these could be costly stained-glass windows or doors. If they are in place, they should be left if they will be suitable for the style and the effect for which you are aiming. Other windows, doors, and more treasures may lie hidden in some storage area, which, according to your preference, may be retained or sold.

If you are purely modernizing a house, you may wish to sell some or all of the stained-glass. This is no problem; antique dealers will gladly take it off your hands. However, consider the decision carefully as that item may be one of the strongest selling points of your house.

Likewise, there could be pieces of furniture pushed aside in the basement, the attic, or in other places. These also can be sold to a used-furniture dealer or to an antique shop. Be careful though: underneath a dozen coats of varnish, you might uncover rare rosewood, teak or other valuable woods. The underneath of a heavily moulded door may reveal solid cypress (an expensive, hard-to-find wood used in old Southern houses). Other finds are forgotten stacks of exterior and interior shutters, doors or mantels that, if not used in the renovation, can yield an unexpected "windfall profit."

Many of these items could be cleaned, strip-dipped and used in this house or in another.

Also, a bonanza in hidden treasures could be boxes of books and vintage magazines. An old *Superman* comic book might be lurking in an attic cache. Peek in every nook and cranny before you fill the dumpster.

---

[17]In one renovation project, the authors came upon a "growing treasure" in the yard. Grounds, well-landscaped but uncared for, were profuse with border plantings of variegated liriope (in the South known as monkey grass). In some places the borders were two to three-feet wide. Calling in a landscape-nursery specialist, they had him divide the large clumps of monkey grass, replanting the borders. The liriope provided a bonus: money was saved by replanting and rearranging the overgrown border and enough plants were left to create an inventory for a parallel project.

Outside Tear-downs

Outside, there may be tool sheds, storage sheds, and garages that at one time were a part of homesteads. Most are in such poor condition that to repair them would cost more than replacement. If it is possible to repair them with a minimum investment, do so, giving them new coats of paint. When they are in an unsalvageable condition, have them torn down and the debris hauled away. The important point to remember is that you must do one or the other. Leaving a wreck of an out-building will detract from the property's good effect and reduce a prospective buyer's interest.[18] On the other hand, a restored garage is a plus.

"Before" And "After"

When you began the renovation, if you remembered to snap a few "before" photographs of your house, now is the time to finish the roll with some dazzling "after" shots. "During" photos will also provide interesting memoirs.

[18] Such yard structures have a low priority with the authors, but one very nice exception was made in restoring a small, detached kitchen standing behind a c. 1890 house. The kitchen was in such a disreputable condition that their first instinct was to tear the building down, but the small building was so appealing and so attractive that the more they looked at it, the more they saw intriguing possibilities for its restoration as a small office or as a studio apartment. The kitchen, in its defiance, won as an attached office. In restoring it, they even left the old brick chimney which pierced the center of the structure. The main house was sold to a law firm and the authors sincerely believe that the "little house," as they came to say, served as a tremendous asset in making the sale. The attorneys' immediate reaction to the "little house" was that it would make a perfect combination law library-conference room and could also double as extra office space when required. So it is today.

12 "Turn Ons"

During the renovation process, you will be on the lookout for prospective buyers. Some may be looking for you, eager to watch over your shoulder. Naturally, renovators are anxious to wow others with the progress being made, and it is often tempting to invite a few potential clients in for a sneak preview.

Beware—unless a buyer appears with a check in hand and is on a twenty-four-hour layover en route from London to Tokyo via your town, it is advisable to wait until the structure has been renovated completely before opening the door. When each area of the dwelling appears impeccable, the stage is then set to inspire the individual buyer to think about his/her own personal decorating ideas.

This does not mean that you will not leave some decorating options open. However, small unfinished places or, on the other hand, small details nicely handled, can make a difference as the next two examples expose.

A client, if asked to visualize what the dining room would look like when the remaining strips of wallpaper had been hung, may make a purchase offer that will jolt your imagination. What might he have bid, had it been a week afterward? Never underestimate the impact of events like this.

One group of renovators is fortunate enough to employ Daisy, a professional cleaning person with a flair for detail. It was arranged that she would always be the last person to leave the house before any clients came through. When Daisy cleans a room, it seems brighter, as if grooves and corners have been tended to as carefully as surfaces. Bathroom drain-openings gleam, doorknobs sparkle. Her rooms reflect an extra measure of order that says: "This room is right; everything here belongs." Renovators could call this "The Daisy Touch," which puts icing on the sale.

EXTERIOR CLEAN-UP

1. Trim bushes and hedges; cut away dead or broken tree limbs.
2. Edge sidewalks and driveways.
3. Weed borders and flower beds.
4. Mow lawn; rake and sweep grass clippings.
5. Clean windows of house inside and out.
6. Wipe off doors and exterior window sills.
7. Sweep and wash porches.
8. Sweep and mop carports, patios and garages, if any.

INTERIOR CLEAN-UP

1. Clean ashes from fireplaces; close flues to prevent soot from blowing in; and polish tile or metal surfaces.
2. Clean kitchens and bathrooms thoroughly, with special attention to such surfaces as chrome, stainless steel and tile, to make them shine. (Spray window-cleaner is particularly effective in adding a quick lustre to chrome, metal and porcelain surfaces).
3. Clean mirrors.
4. Polish brass, if any, until it gleams.
5. Check high places and corners for cobwebs.
6. Clean areas on which dust may have settled (mantels, window sills, mouldings, lighting fixtures, doors and newly painted areas).
7. Mop floors until they are spotless (corners, too).
8. Vacuum bare and carpeted floors.

Making The House A "Home"

1. Install good quality, brass or other nice-looking house numbers in a suitable place on the exterior.
2. Put bulbs in all lighting fixtures.
3. If you wish, arrange logs in each open fireplace. (This makes a house look extremely cozy).
4. Though it is best to show a house during daylight hours, if you do show it at night, make sure that porch lights are on and that the lighting is set in each room before the client enters.
5. In a room in which a lighting fixture has not yet been installed (to provide buyer option), use a temporary lamp or flashlight. (It's handy to have a flashlight anyway, for looking around outdoors).
6. Have water, electricity, heat/air conditioning turned on. (Nothing is more disconcerting and uncomfortable than trying to show off a newly painted house, in the dark, to a prospective buyer who is freezing or perspiring profusely).
7. Have commodes operating.
8. Place paper towels, soap and ashtrays in the kitchen utilizing quality toilet tissue and attractive bars of soap in each bathroom.

To keep things ship-shape, breeze through the house between clients. Keep a bottle of window cleaner handy for unexpected finger prints! Tidy up places in which water or ash trays may have been used, check for turned off lights, or closet doors left ajar.

Make it look as if **Daisy** had been there!

13 An Extra Tip or Two

1. **D**o not become involved in a house renovation project unless everyone concerned in the undertaking (husband **and** wife; all members of a business group) is enthusiastic from the beginning. You will need every atom of cooperation, strength, patience, and optimism during the renovation process. Nothing invigorates a project so much as a mutual commitment. A disinterested, unimaginative, unwilling partner (whether spouse, friend or business associate) weakens, delays and stymies progress.

2. **Do not take on more than you can afford** to renovate or, if you are renovating for personal use, more than would be possible for you to maintain. That eighteen-room Georgian structure may seem the house of your dreams, but do you really have the capital to put it in livable condition? Heating and cooling costs alone may be more than your monthly budget can handle.

3. Do first tasks first. Do not start painting and hanging expensive wallpaper in a house that has a leaking roof. A faulty heating system and outdated wiring could cause a fire. Those

broken water pipes and a wornout plumbing system can destroy your initial hard work.

4. **Use professional help.** There is nothing wrong in being a do-it-yourselfer. You will find enough to do, even if you have minimum skills. Do not take chances in areas in which you have no competence or that are dangerous or very costly.

5. **Do what you can:** cleaning, yard work, painting—especially painting if you are on a limited renovation budget. Most people can paint, and the cost of such labor is very expensive. A guideline to estimate the cost of painting various type surfaces can be obtained from any reputable paint dealer.

6. **You can learn to do a lot if you have to.** Just because you understand little about carpentry, electricity, or plumbing does not mean that you cannot learn.[19] Not to be forgotten is the importance of having a professional electrician and plumber inspect all work. And another warning is in order here: a license is required in many skilled trades; and building codes may demand professional labor. These protect your safety and can be the law as well.

7. Priorities differ considerably in **renovating a house for yourself** over a place for lease or sale.

If it is your residence and you are on a limited renovation budget, you **can** live with some sound but slightly outdated bathroom fixtures or a 1950's kitchen. Paint, wallpaper and fabrics work wonders in cosmetically updating a vintage bathroom or kitchen, enabling you to reserve your limited funds for the more necessary projects. Those left undone can be remodeled later when more funds are available.

Renovating for lease or sale is an entirely different matter. Most prospective buyers will expect a modern kitchen and bathrooms. An outdated home may cost you a sale.

8. In the renovation process, **do not buy costly equipment** that you might not use enough to justify the expense. Of course, if you are purchasing a three-story house to renovate and plan to live there for the rest of your life, it may be wise to acquire such items as a set of extension ladders. It is best, though, to purchase only things that will prove valuable over the long term; especially avoid

---

[19] A friend of the authors, who has renovated several houses and who describes himself as a "technical novice," studied several carpentry manuals before he began any renovation. He did all the carpentry on his first house, contracting out the plumbing and electrical work. In the interval before beginning his second renovation, he took an electrical course, enabling him to assist in the wiring on the second project.

new, untested, or fad equipment. The old methods are often more reliable.

Renting equipment is usually the best; rental businesses are well supplied and their prices, while not inexpensive, may be the best route for such items as floor sanders and waxers.

9. **Consider your neighbors' feelings** despite having to do essential tasks first. Replace the leaking roof, damaged siding, a faulty heating system, and outdated wiring and plumbing, but as soon as possible have the exterior painted and the yard in shape. Do not make the neighbors wait and stew while you fashion the interior into one from *House Beautiful.* They will not like having to continue looking at your house with its flaking, faded paint and yard filled with debris. (In the past, these conditions have most probably deflated the value of their own homes). Bear in mind that if the house will be your residence, they will be **your** neighbors.

Quite aside from that aspect anyway, friendship with your neighbors is most important—using their phone in an emergency, borrowing a tool or a piece of equipment, appreciating them while utilizing them as unofficial, unpaid "watch persons" during the renovation process while the house is unoccupied and vandalism and theft are a real threat. Most will have their own opinions about your property, however, and you will hear these ideas frequently. Listen to them intently, thank them for their superb help, and then make your own decisions.

10. **Renovation or restoration.** This must be decided early; sometimes there is no choice. If you purchase a house listed on *The National Register of Historic Places,* or one in a local historic district or one protected by a local Preservation Society, you may be required to restore the building as nearly to the original as is possible. This requirement normally refers only to the exterior; you will probably be allowed to make interior changes as you wish to adapt the structure to modern use.

Know what kind of property you are purchasing beforehand; do not depend upon the verbal assurances of the seller unless he is willing to put the statement in writing under the signature of local preservation groups that "the house is not protected by restrictions." Restoration is a much more expensive proposition than renovation and, if necessary, will probably increase your costs substantially.

11. **Utilize free advice without hesitation.** Advice, "free for the asking," abounds. When you are buying any item, whether it is a lighting fixture, a plumbing product, or paint, do not be shy

about asking questions. Talk only with competent professionals. Most are pleased to show off their expertise, and give you free advice.

You may have heard the story of the fellow who hired a carpet installer for four hours, meanwhile receiving a short course in how-to-install carpet himself. Now, that home-renovator—when he needs to install carpet—buys it on sale, rents installer's equipment, and completes the task alone.

Any other individual could use the same idea in learning how to install plaster board or vinyl floor-covering. Nevertheless, if funds are available, the better choice is to have a professional do the work, even though inventiveness and your own labor can extend a limited budget.

Critical, too, are the costs of interest, insurance, taxes, and other non-profitable expenses that are occurring while your renovation is slowed. The do-the-job-yourself may effect savings on the one hand but they can be offset by other costs.

Naturally, this problem is of more concern in a firm's renovation business than with a personal dwelling.

12. **Renovation for psychological effect.** A do-the-job-yourselfer, one who has renovated several houses, passed along a hint that could be applicable in every situation. His group had almost given up on its very first house-project because, as hard as they worked, all areas still seemed to be half-done. No room was finished—everywhere there appeared to be twenty different projects needing completion. Finally, they uncovered the secret after he and his wife worked out a schedule of priorities. Now, initially on a house renovation, they accomplish required necessities; then they "move in," and follow the rule of exterior beautification before tackling the house one room at a time. This may not work for everyone, but generally is more progressive. Little by little, parts of the house are totally completed; there is no demoralizing vision of an entire house done only partially. Too, if **any** visitors are allowed in, the impact is greater. Friends, in that instance, will ask questions and put forth their ideas on the areas still to be restored. Keep the idea in mind.

13. **Selling for profit.** Emotions are perilous factors in selling any house; for instance, to someone who may have grown up there. Because of such attachment, that person may believe the structure has more value than it really does. The same feelings come into being when you are selling the renovated house into which you have put a great deal of planning, hard work and money

during the two to six-month period of restoration, especially if it was the first you did.

You must be realistic in establishing the fair-market appraisal price, and try to sell at that price regardless of the ensuing emotional trauma.

14. **Be careful and mindful of safety,** should you be renovating by yourself. Essential items are safety glasses, proper shoes, gloves and other equipment, not only for safety but also from an efficiency standpoint. Additionally, always be on the lookout for hazards that could cause personal injury or property damage.

"Going Pro"

14 Accounting

Introduction to accounting. Following financial stability, accounting and proper record-keeping are the next critical elements on your path to a successful renovation operation. The truth is, if you do not keep accurate accounts, you cannot know whether you are stable monetarily. You may quickly learn that your funds are depleted and you have no choice but to end the venture. Under no circumstances should you believe that all of the facts and figures can be kept in your memory, in your pocket, in the glove compartment of your car, or in a "shoe box" file.

A detailed accounting history, from the beginning, is imperative to tell your position at any given time, where you have been, and where you are going. This is necessary both internally and for your accountant, attorney and banker. Obviously, well-kept records maximize success in meeting your local, state and federal tax obligations with a minimum of effort.

In this chapter there are sample one-month accounting records. The focus is on specific breakdowns in the General Ledger regarding typical houses that were purchased, renovated and sold. Details are shown for all expenses involved, as this is necessary to calculate the net profit after the house is sold. While many properties can yield higher profits than those "typical examples" shown here, these will serve to explain the record-keeping in a practical way.

EXAMPLE 1

GENERAL OPERATING LEDGER

You will note from the accounting table in Example 1 that this method is neither so sophisticated nor so complex. Even the non-analytical individual will be able to understand.[20] It is a simple system devised to expand checkbook entries into meaningful categories.

The basic premise is that the accounting sheet balance always agrees with the checkbook balance. The checkbook balance in turn is reconciled each month against the bank statement. In this manner, it is possible to double-check against mistakes.

You may have several bank accounts for the purpose of separating certain projects, satisfying lending requirements for a specific property, or various other reasons. No matter how many bank accounts, the procedure is exactly the same, requiring every item from each account to be entered on one General Ledger sheet. The "balance" on the General Ledger will equal the total of the balances in your checkbook(s).

This ledger offers an overall accounting view at any one time. It shows the amount of capital, operating expenses, office expenses, the "offer money" outstanding, expenditures on each project and so on, in addition to brief explanations of any of the above when necessary. This sheet or one similar is essential. Once-a-week posting insures knowledge of all expenditures for each project. If you should choose this sample or any other form of accounting, you **must** post at the minimum of once a month, but more frequently is advised.

In the next few paragraphs, the columns on the General Ledger are further explained. Remember that it is essential to have a separate column for each renovation job. This can readily reveal the total invested on a specific project which will assist in reaching decisions about further expenditures.

---

[20]The authors' firm, Curry-Jones, keeps renovation records in a manner similar to the ledger sheet in this chapter. This system has worked well for them, even with multi-bank accounts. For example, rather than use a more extensive ledger, they find it beneficial to be able to tally a year's expenses in such categories as postage, entertainment, etc., into general office expenses. At year's end these are manually broken down according to the category of expenditure.

Example 1

Pg. 18

Prepared By
Approved By
Initials Date

XYZ Company
1978 General Operating Ledger

* (Name changed here to protect individuals)

Item	Ck #	Date 1978	Capital Account	Gen. off expense	Telephone expense	Interest, Insurance	Offers Made	47 South St	1082 Man St	1182 Indian Rd	481 Service	247 Lake Rd	Book	Balance (checkbook)	Explanation
FORM SUBTOTALS			9469¹⁹	5503⁸⁸	2526²²	1491—	2000—	1149²³	(45-)	5⁴⁵	39711⁵⁵	39207⁸⁷	893⁷⁸	8583⁸⁷	
Palmetto Hdwr.	1130	8/37										36⁴¹			Rent for office space
Lowes	1131	8/29		125—								21			Brother fee-leaving
Continental R.I.	113a	9/1	110⁵⁰												Misc. carpentry
Dep - Services, Inc															
P.M. Williams	132	9/12			(69⁴⁵)						45—				Personal phone calls paid
Dep - Partner Y	1	9/1					1000—								Earnest money - 2712 Ave. A.
McFarr	1133	9/4			36⁰⁰					5⁰⁰					Water changes - 1 mo
Forest Acres	1134	9/5													
Answer phone	1135	9/5													Brokerage lease fee
Dep-WWZZ fee		9/5	750⁰⁰												Disbursed above - split?
Internal Partner X	333	9/5	(375⁰⁰)												(equal $6: 50-50)
$ Partner Y	334	9/5	(375⁰⁰)												Floors refinished
W.C. Chopland	1136	9/5										5³⁰			Reimb. - photos
Partner Z	1137	9/7									400—	1000—		668⁷⁵	Work done per invoice
C.M. Portman	1138	9/7		20⁶⁵											Tool/nylon tape
Piedmont Printers	1139	9/8													Electrical work
Will_ Mangum	1140	9/8													Payment on 2nd Mortgage
IAM Property. Dep		9/8								5⁰⁰	48⁰⁰	5⁰⁰			Additional premium
Delmons, Ins Ag	1141	9/13													Fix toilet
Chalgren Plbg.	1143	9/3		8⁰⁹							32⁷⁰				Reimb. - postage due
Partner Z	1143	9/3		15—								36—			100 stamps
Postmaster	1144	9/13													Offer refused
Void ck #1133	1145	9/15					(1000-)					3180—			Permit for work
City of Columbia															New roof
All Weather Roof & Tile	1146	9/15													Donation-crippled children
Jamil Shone	1147	9/18		37⁵⁰		779¹⁷						400—			Carpentry repairs
C.M. Portman	1148	9/18													Interest on note
ABC Bank	1149	9/18										50—			Cleaning
C. Greene	1150	9/19		10—											
B. Davison	1151	9/19		10—											
C. Greene	115a	9/19													Earnest on 1481 Tuxedo Rd
McFarr	1153	9/20													Phone
Sou. Bell	1154	9/21			335⁴³								236⁹⁹		Case - electric
SCEG = 44.18	1155	9/21			44						6⁸⁶	37—			To expense: pd cash - Kent
Petty Cash		9/27	110⁵⁰	(38⁵⁸)						3¹²		35—			Brother elec
Dep - Services, Inc	1	9/27													Another elec
Dep - Net proceeds		9/27	7248⁰⁸								7296⁶⁸				Sale of house
Internal adjustment		9/27									(4759⁶⁵)				To put profit into account
TOTALS			107111⁸⁷	5399⁹⁴	2698³⁶	2263¹⁷	4000—	999⁷⁹	(45-)	8⁵⁷	0—	49256³⁹	893⁷⁸	47893⁹⁵	

Capital Account

Please note in Example 1 that the Capital Account records the flow of capital. The Capital Account reflects all capital investments (money that any partner subscribes to the business), profits made on houses, rental income, notes payable (funds borrowed), income from any other source (i.e., broker leasing fees in this company's case) that are being funneled through the business. The Capital Account also reflects such out-go of capital as payment of notes or any disbursement to a partner. As a matter of reference, all entries that are bank-deposited are entered here as a positive figure and all disbursements in parentheses, indicating a "minus" for column-total purposes. Lines 5 and 11 of column 2 (Example 1) represent fees earned on another side-line business. The fee was entered into the Capital Account because it represents an additional source of income.

While the Capital Account appears very simple on the General Ledger sheet, it is actually very complicated and of great interest to "Uncle Sam." Hence, it is necessary to have a complete breakdown on a supplementary ledger (Example 2), not only of each source of income and disbursement, but also of each partner's individual share in the overall total. You may find this (Example 2) to be the most difficult ledger to keep. However, you will develop your own methods, perhaps easier ones, as time passes and more familiarity with the business occurs.

Offers Made
And Individual Project Expenditures

In Example 1, the entries correspond to checks drawn. They are entered as a positive amount with any deposits against these expenses written as a negative amount for the column's total.

You will note a column (Example 1, column 13) titled "Book." Expenses here have been separated so that costs may be tabulated on a yearly running basis. You could do the same with any special project, even contract-jobs, should you enter that field.

Line 8, column 6 (Example 1), "offers made": Always note property address in the explanation column like the sample ones shown here. If you have several checks for offers outstanding, figures can become confused easily unless noted with addresses.

Line 15, column 11 (Example 1): Most firms keep petty cash

on hand at all times for small expenditures but, invariably, a member will be away from the office and find a need to pay cash for some purpose. If he has a "cash receipt" to verify the expenditure, that person is reimbursed.

Column 7 (Example 1) represents a renovated house on which a second mortgage was accepted for the balance due after the first mortgage had been assumed by a purchaser (all these accounting transactions took place prior to this page's entries). An investment in the house, still held, is listed under the category of "projects," though it is not deeded in the firm's name. Each monthly payment (line 19) shows as a deposit against the investment, reducing the same.

Column 8 (Example 1): The figure shown here is a minus one, but the project actually has an "income balance." More expenditures are expected to be charged against this money. (The house had been sold, but all bills and/or expense statements had not yet been received). Most of the income had previously been disbursed, however.

Column 9 (Example 1): Same case as in column 8, except here the expenditures were larger than income at this point. (In both the Indian and Main Street houses, the profits had already been punched into the Capital Account and distributed). The figures in both columns 8 and 9 represent the residues.

Column 10 (Example 1): With the project's completion during the month, the net proceeds of the sale were entered on line 38. The total of the figure preceding line 39 was the net profit (not shown). All of the expenses had been carried until the time of the sale, so the difference between money invested and payment received at the time of closing was the profit. Line 39, column 2, shows an "internal transfer" (no check written or deposit received) to the Capital Account for the amount of the profit. This is a routine procedure in this type of accounting system. At the time of closing, some purchases had not been billed; however, a refund of the unearned premium on the homeowner's insurance would more than cover the delayed billings for expenses (column 8 and 9 are examples of houses in this time frame). When every item will have been paid or refunded, the balance will be transferred to the Capital Account and disbursed accordingly. Therefore, the house listed in column 10 will be deleted from the next General Ledger sheet.

Column 11 (Example 1): A project just getting underway; in reality, renovation of a larger, more costly house than that in column 10, the Seville Road property.

Balance

After posting all deposits and checks in the checkbook(s), total each column (as in Example 1). To find the "balance" for the balance column, punch in the Capital Account as a plus, then subtract each of the other columns (unless there is a figure in parentheses, in which case it should be added in order to show the opposite of an expense item). This process will give you the "balance." To double-check, make sure this balance is the sum total of all checkbook balances. It is very important to double-check totals each time you post to save time and headaches later.

Summary

As for "General Ledger Accounting," it really is just an expansion and summary of your checkbook(s), noting monetary activity in a more useful and meaningful form. The task may be accomplished in numbers of ways, but the results will be essentially the same.

If desired, there can be Back-up sheets for any column on the General Ledger. It is wise to have Back-up Journals for the Capital Account (Example 2) and one for each renovation project (Example 3) to provide essential, quick information. The Capital Account Journal reveals income figures to be used at year-end for tax information; the renovation-project sheet shows cost figures on each type of work done.

EXAMPLE 2

CAPITAL ACCOUNT BREAKDOWN

As mentioned before, this ledger breaks down all income and disbursements of capital into the source. At a quick glance during the year, you can see how much taxable income has been received by adding columns 3 through 6. These columns, along with 7 and 8, are the most important items on this page.

Capital Contributed

The "capital contributed" (column 2) represents all funds invested by partners. A check or cash deposited in the company ac-

Example 2

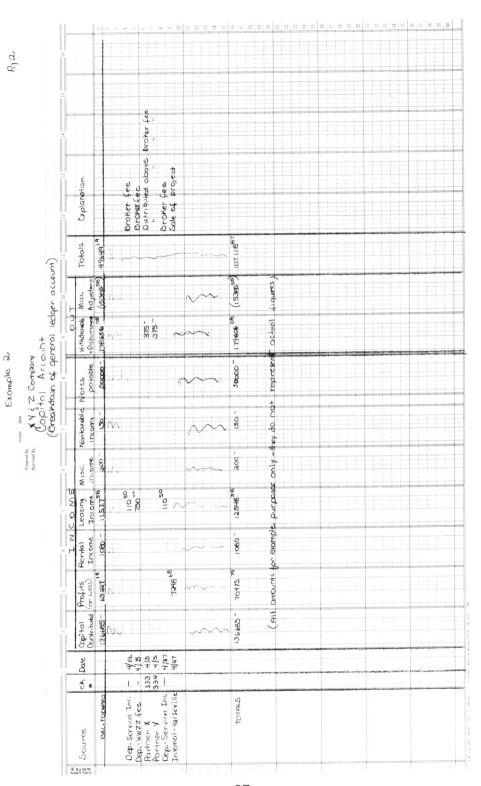

count from a partner's own funds is listed here. (The partner may have obtained these funds from a number of sources, i.e., personal bank or savings account, individual note, a personal loan, etc.). Hence, the column represents in-flow of a partner's own funds.

Profits

As stated, gross profit is the difference between the amount you receive when you sell a property, minus the total investment, including expenditures. How to figure profit is indicated, for example, in a property like the Seville Road house:

Amount paid for house	$36,000.00
Repairs and renovation costs	4,297.83
Total investment	$40,297.83

Sold for	$51,500.00
Less costs, from closing statement [not shown]	3,953.49
Net (closing check)	$47,546.51
Less total investment (Above)	$40,297.83
Profit (Line 39, Example 1, columns 2 and 10)	$ 7,248.68

Any future expenses or income on this house would be handled in the General Operating Ledger in the same manner, with the final figure being transferred to the Capital Account to be recorded as income or, if by misfortune, a loss. If those profits were not split 50-50 between partners, you would need several columns here, depending on the number of partners. (The same goes for columns 4-10).

Rental Income

Column 4 represents any rental income the firm might have received. You need to break away rentals from other income, as rental income is not subject to FICA taxes at the present time.

Leasing Income

Column 5 represents income from a specific sideline business. This could be any endeavor that passes through the checkbook(s) used. The company received broker fees for putting together leasing packages, as the $750 entry indicates.

Miscellaneous Income

"Miscellaneous Income" is a catch-all category for other, seldom recurring income figures. There could be fees for a lecture, an article written for a magazine or a book, referral of a contractor to an individual or vice versa, a contract renovation job for an individual, or a consulting fee.

Nontaxable Income

Column 7 records security deposits that are refundable when a rental-property occupant moves. These are nontaxable to a firm or individual as it is not your money—the funds belong to someone else.

Notes Payable

This column (8) represents funds borrowed in the business' name for the various projects. It is always good (and necessary) to know what you owe.

Withdrawals And Disbursements

Any check written to a partner as a disbursement from any source, i.e., profits, rental income, other types of income, or even a "divy" up of notes payable until such times as they are needed to be contributed back to the business for expenses (entered in column 2 then) is shown here. The IRS requires you to list this as an item on your tax return in most cases, unless you are an individual proprietor.

Column 10: "Miscellaneous Adjustment" falls into the same "accounting purposes only" category. Here, the figure represents retained earnings from the previous year. All business operating expenses (columns 3, 4, 5, Example 1) for the preceding year had been closed out to this account, with the new year beginning with a zero balance.

Totals

Column 11 is the sum of columns 2-8 in income, less columns 9-10 in disbursements and adjustments. This should always balance with the total of column 2, Capital Account, in the General Operating Ledger (Example 1). Once Back-up Journals are set up properly, you will find them extremely valuable tools in your business. Keep in mind that they can be adjusted to any type of operation.

EXAMPLE 3

PROJECT EXPENSES

The Project Expenses Ledger is of great importance to any firm or individual renovating for a profit, as well as the person restoring for his or her own use. It is simply a breakdown of expenditures incurred during the process of property rehabilitation. Each project will vary and there will be differences in costs involved. Generally, you will have to undertake purchases or repairs for each project for heating and air conditioning, roofing, insulation, sheet rock, plaster, plumbing, wiring, floor coverings, tile, painting, and other restorations.

It is helpful to break the expenditure columns down into the more costly items in each particular renovation as you will note in columns 3-12. There are small or zero balances in some columns at the project's end, yet these are items normally common to every job. All items were checked on the particular project but some were neither in need of repair nor upgrading and others required only minor expenditures. This was a renovation demanding more sprucing up, modernizing, and cleaning, rather than repairing or replacing. Most projects require such extensive repairs that a "quickie" like this would certainly be refreshing.

Example 3

Prepared By _____ Initials ____ Date ____
Approved By _____

XYZ Company
421 Seville Road
(Project expenses)

Source	ck #	Date 1978	Purchase Price	Heating + A/C	Roofing	Painting	Wallpaper/decorative	Insulation	Sheetrock/Plaster	Carpentry	Plumbing	Electrical + fixtures	Carpeting/Floors Refinished	Misc.	Balance	Explanation
Delmons Int. Agency	1071	6/69												105-		Insurance
E. Richland Co.	1084	7/1												13.20		Water bill (+ sewer)
GAM-attorneys = 33986.81	3317	7/2	36000.00											3-		Purchase price
"	"	"												.35		Record deed
"	"	"														Title search
	—	7/3												(141.19)		Proration tx 1978 taxes
Petty cash		7/3												32.25		Cleaning supplies
Al McDougal	1092	7/20												49		Clean out - labor - etc.
Tompkins Paint	1095	7/24														Wallpaper
O. Moore	1096	7/24					148.64									Painting draw
C.M. H+q + A/C	1100	7/30		650.00		1115-									38732.73	Repair thermostat + check
SCE+G	1101	7/30												7.43		Elec. + Gas
O. Moore	3321	7/07												2.98		Painting draw
C.H. of Forest Acres	1105	8/1														Water
P.M. Williams	1107	8/3							170-	75-						Minor repairs
C.B. Murray	1101	8/3														Plaster patching
W.R. Rogers	1111	8/7														Wallpaper hanging 18 s/r
Cap. Electric	1114	8/7										20.66				Kitchen light fix.
F. Portman	1114	8/8											388-			Vinyl or carpet installed
Petty cash		8/10														Misc. repair items
Cash	—													69.64		Scotch plate, etc.
Chalgreen Plbg	1116	8/21									58.95			48.39		Repairs
B. Davison	1119	9/21												40-		Cleaning - interior
SCE+G	1123	9/21												17.78		Elec. + Gas
Film, Inc.	1125	9/27												9.20		Pictures printed
Palmetto Hdwr.	1130	8/27												36.91		Hinges, pulls, etc.
Lowes	1131	8/28								45-				2.81		Misc. clamps, etc.
P.M. Williams	3333	9/21														Misc. carpentry
Forest Acres	104	9/15									22.78	48-	400-	5.00		Water
W.C. Chapland	1136	9/5														Floors refinished + skimmed
Will Mangum	1140	9/6														Elec. repairs
Chalgreen Plbg.	1143	9/21														Fix toilet
SCE+G	1155	9/21												6.84	40887.83	Elec. + gas
TOTALS			36000-	650.00	0	2315.00	538.64	0	170.00	120-	81.65	68.66	788-	450.38	40817.83	

Make sure that column 14 (balance) of this ledger agrees with the total on the General Operating Ledger for this project. For example, the balance $40,297.83 (column 14) is the balance of column 10, General Operating Ledger (Example 1), as posted through line 35. Actually, the $40,297.83 is not shown per se but can easily be calculated by subtracting line 39 from line 38. Usually, the net proceeds check is not recorded on the Project Ledger, though such a column could be added. If reference to this ledger is required at a later date, it is usually for expense items and is not checked for income or profit figures. Income is recorded on the other two ledgers (General Operating and Capital Account).

Accounting Chapter Summary

The ledgers mentioned above are basic outlines of the method of keeping up with income and expenditures. Shown here are all of the necessary records. You may individualize them to your needs in a way you prefer.

From time to time it is well to do a summary on renovations completed to determine how much certain jobs and materials have cost, so as to be able to project future expenses. For this, pick up the totals in each expense column from the project sheets. To cite one very revealing expenditure, on the three simulated renovations here, heating/air conditioning costs were $8,240.20, broken down as follows: Seville, $65.20 (only minor repairs); Main Street, $4500 (new system); and Indian Road, $3675 (new system, smaller house). An example of this type of summary is not shown, but is easy for anyone to set up.

When first looking at a property for renovation, it is extremely valuable to be able to approximate the cost of repairs. Accounting accuracy is essential throughout a specific project and will also parallel your firm's entire path to success.

15 "In Business"

One of the initial steps prior to starting in business will be to determine whether you will operate as a proprietorship, a partnership, or a corporation.

A **proprietorship** is an exclusive legal right to be in business for a definite or indefinite period of time.

A **partnership** is a legal relationship existing between two or more persons associated contractually as joint principals in a business.

A **corporation** is a body formed and authorized to act as a single person, although constituted by one or more persons, and legally endowed with various rights and duties, including the capacity of succession.

Though proprietorships, partnerships and corporations are somewhat the same, they have many varying degrees of differences. When beginning your renovation venture, a sole proprietorship may be best. As your firm grows, you may take in partners, or become a corporation, depending upon the various tax incentives, profit goals and available time you have for the business.

Whatever operation you think you might choose, you will need to have several conferences with your accountant, attorney, and insurance agent to review the pros and cons of the proper business structure.

There is no set answer for every person. However, with careful examination of your circumstances and competent advice, you should be able to determine the best answer.

In reference to those necessary licenses, the first move is **find out the rules.** Most cities, municipalities and counties require a Business License, quite possibly a General Contractor's License, and a Permit for work to be done on each particular job. Since there are varying regulations throughout the country, you should check in your local area to determine which are required for your purposes. Possibly, if you renovate just one home or another type property for an investment, there will be no business license, contractor's license, or permit needed. If you renovate several homes, you may fall into the category of an operating business and may be required to follow the applicable regulations and rules.

In review, be sure to comply with the local regulations as you want to be a respected member of the business community and will certainly desire to act accordingly.

In Review

Restore Your Future can indeed be a profit guide to property renovation. This book directs you toward future successful ventures on an individual or an investment basis.

You will begin with property selection; go into the actual purchase, which includes contracts, closing statements, legal counsel, financing, insurance and tax tips; then learn about the various phases of renovation such as plumbing, heating/air conditioning, electrical, decorating, painting and landscaping. The detailed checklists you will find are also very helpful. Finally, accounting permits, licenses, and other pertinent phases of running a business are outlined.

This business can be a career, a one-time investment, or the renovation of your own home or other property. There can be incredible opportunities and rewards in renovation and restoration. High on the list of advantages are civic pride and personal financial gains. As quoted in the July, 1980, issue of *Money Magazine*, "A study by *Building Supply News* found that the number of home improvement projects undertaken each year in the U.S. has increased a startling 52% since 1972." Only a fraction of the vast inventory of properties has been restored.

In review, there are interesting challenges and unlimited future earnings-potential to be found in this business. The final decisions are yours; however, with the benefit of the knowledge gained here, your path to success will be greatly enhanced.

JACK BIRNEY CURRY, JR.

Native of Atlanta, Georgia.
Graduated with BBA in 1964 from the University of Georgia.

CAREER EXPERIENCE:

United States Air Force and insurance business — 1965-1969.
Insurance-pension plans, leasing companies — 1970-1976.
Since 1976, engaged actively in renovation and restoration of historic properties and other real estate developments. An owner of Curry & Company, Realtors, Columbia, South Carolina, and a financial broker dealing in varied equipment loans/leases on commercial and industrial applications.

SHIRLEY FLANAGAN CURRY

Native of West Palm Beach, Florida.
Graduated with BBA in 1964 from Emory University.
Graduate courses in math and education.

CAREER EXPERIENCE:

Taught school in Atlanta (math) for three and one-half years.
Income tax returns for two years in Columbia, South Carolina.
Accountant for small corporation for two years.
Since 1976, engaged actively in renovation and restoration of historic properties and other real estate developments. Also, an owner of Curry & Company, Realtors, Columbia, South Carolina. Handles all accounting tasks and coordinates the decoration on renovation projects.

MARKLEY LEE JONES

Native of Atlanta, Georgia.
Graduated with BBA in 1960 from the University of Georgia.

CAREER EXPERIENCE:

Fifteen years experience in the banking, financial and leasing field with emphasis on marketing and management.
Since 1976, engaged actively in renovation and restoration of historic properties and other real estate developments; partner in Curry-Jones, Columbia, South Carolina. Owner of Markley Lee Jones Real Estate, Atlanta, Georgia; also, a financial broker, dealing primarily in varied equipment loans/leases on commercial and industrial applications.